AWFUL FIRST DATES

AWFUL FIRST DATES

Hysterical, True, and Heartbreakingly Bad

SARAH Z. WEXLER

sourcebooks
casablanca

Published by Sourcebooks Casablanca, an imprint of Sourcebooks, Inc.
P.O. Box 4410, Naperville, Illinois 60567-4410
(630) 961-3900
Fax: (630) 961-2168
www.sourcebooks.com

Library of Congress Cataloging-in-Publication Data

Wexler, Sarah Z. (Sarah Zoe)
  Awful first dates : hysterical, true, and heartbreakingly bad / Sarah Z. Wexler.
     p. cm.
  Includes bibliographical references and index.
  (pbk. : alk. paper) 1. Dating (Social customs)--Anecdotes. I. Title.
  HQ801.W652 2012
  306.73--dc23
                          2011035362

Printed and bound in the United States of America.
VP 10 9 8 7 6 5 4 3 2 1

Here's to great couples, who give me hope,
and to great singles, who also give me hope.

CONTENTS

Awful First Date: Hollywood Dispatch

"I was a smart dating girl. I always had enough money for a cab from wherever I was. I didn't have any problem breaking a date. Like I'd say, 'You know what, this date is really not working out. Don't worry—if you don't pick up the tab, I will, and I'll take a cab back to my house.' If you say it like you mean it, the dates can't be bad—they just end."

—Wendy Williams

Awful First Date: Hollywood Dispatch

"Most of my dates have been pretty messed-up."
—Taylor Momsen

INTRODUCTION

ecently I was interviewing Cindy Crawford for a magazine article, and as much as I wanted to focus on hearing about the ingredients in her new skin-care line, I couldn't stop thinking about the bad date I'd had the night before. A really bad date, especially one you'd had high hopes for, can rock your self-esteem and leave you feeling hopeless, not only about dating, but also about love—and on a dramatic day, about humanity in general. So at the end of our chat, I asked her if she had ever been out with a toad. She thought for a moment and then told me she's "never been on a really bad date." Right. Of course she hasn't. When I asked Jennifer Lopez the same question, she told me, "I was never a dater. I had a boyfriend from the time I was sixteen until I was twenty-three, and then I got married. I never did the date scene—I was lucky."

Cindy Crawford, Jennifer Lopez: this book is not for you.

It's for the rest of us. For those of us who think we are perfectly normal (or at least normal-ish), yet somehow keep meeting guys who are drunk, weird, rude, pushy, or critical, who lack basic human communication skills, who are not actually single, or who try to hump our legs before we even order appetizers. Our theme song is a mash-up of Three 6 Mafia's "It's Hard out Here for a Pimp" and Beyoncé's "Single Ladies (Put a Ring on It)," something adding up to "It's Hard out Here for All the Single Ladies." And is it ever. Even if you're happily paired off now, you probably went on a bad date, or have friends telling you their weekly Saturday-night horror stories, so this book is for you too. It's for all of us who've gone on bad set-ups, bad Internet dates, dates where you wish your whole life was filmed so you could turn to the camera in a private aside, mid-date, like Ferris Bueller or Zack Morris or Michael Scott, and mouth, "Really?" This book is for all of us who have gone into a date hoping to find Mr. Right and instead met Mr. Cheapskate, Mr. Drunk-Before-Noon, or Mr. Told-Me-I'm-Fat.

The thing is, I can't entirely hold Cindy Crawford's comment against her, because I used to be in that camp. Not that I mean I was a superhot international supermodel who had boys gawking at me in Pepsi commercials or anything, but just that I didn't always have trouble with men; I wasn't always going on bad dates. In fact, until my midtwenties, I'd always been someone's girlfriend. I'm not sure I'd even *been on* a date—I just met someone and he became my boyfriend, the way that so many young people do. Dates with complete strangers were for people on *The Bachelor* or in romantic comedies. Instead, I've basically been paired up since the third grade (seeing *Beethoven* with Michael Duarte, the kid with the blonde bowl cut and the really cool purple Umbros—swoon!). I was in one relationship for three years in high school, another for four years in college (it ended when I studied abroad and found an international boyfriend), and the one after that lasted for three years. I never let one guy go until I'd lined up the next sucker—er, suitor.

Which is why it shocked everyone when I decided to

break up with a boyfriend *without* a backup guy waiting in the wings. Nope, I was ready to try something fun and casual—going on dates! It seemed so cosmopolitan. I couldn't wait to get a manicure, glide on some red lipstick, and meet a stranger in a candle-lit restaurant for a glass of wine. After all, there had to be millions of single men in my new home, New York City. But first I had to meet them. In college, people met prospective dates in class, in intramural sports, or the next morning when they woke up in the same bed after a keg party. But postacademia, it gets tougher to date people you know, unless you make a move on a coworker, your mailman, or the guy who delivers your Chinese food. And not having a network of vouched-for men means a lot of random set-ups and Internet dating sites. Which means strangers, basically. And as I quickly learned, it also means lowering your expectations. Instead of those romantic candle-lit dinners, I got a guy whose idea of a picnic spread, after a five-mile hike, was pulling out a half-full baggie of trail mix.

I spent the next three years going on first dates—and a couple seconds, and even a few fourths. By the end, I had my routine down: blow-dry my hair, lacquer on the eye makeup, pop in a mint, and be on my way. Ever since

I approached the wrong guy at a coffee shop, thinking he was my Internet date, I always got to the meeting place early so it would be up to him to recognize me. If anyone would have to be embarrassed before the date even started, it would be him. While I'd wait, I'd sit and text my male friend the info I had about my date, like his username or where he told me he worked (my friend requested this, I think, because he watched too much *Law & Order: SVU*).

But once the guy would show up and we'd get to talking, my funny, sprawling stories—about a horrible coworker, my psycho former roommate, snorkeling in Barbados—became reduced to pat one-liners I recited to man after man. I went on so many dates, answering the same questions so many times, that I would sometimes pause, midsentence, not remembering if I'd just made the joke about my boss to this guy five minutes ago or if that was the guy I saw on Tuesday. It was exhausting, disheartening, and occasionally a good time, but nothing stuck. Either I didn't like him, or he didn't like me, or we mutually disliked each other. I just couldn't seem to find the win-win opposite of that. I wasn't asking for love at first sight—just like after first date.

So I kept trying. Somehow I got the idea that it was

about controlling outside variables, and so for the next seven first dates I went on, I chose the same restaurant. Still nothing. Then I widened my scope. I went out with a special-ed teacher, a veterinarian, an investment banker, a divorcé still hung up on his ex, a coworker, one of my former college professors, a cop, a musician, a lawyer, an architect, a Peace Corps volunteer, and a few fellow magazine writers and editors. I suffered countless awkward good-byes on street corners, including one where the guy looked at the spray bottle on my keychain, which my dad bought me as a housewarming gift when I first moved to New York, and asked if I would Mace him if he tried to kiss me. (He did. I should have.) I tried to keep a straight face when the haughty Shakespearean actor confessed his day job for the past decade: donning the furry head of the city's back-flipping baseball mascot.

I realize it wasn't *all* the guys' fault. I mean, I'm not exactly Cindy Crawford or J.Lo (but my mom tells me I'm close!). I'm sure I scared off more than a few potential suitors by talking about how I dressed my dog up as a lobster for Halloween and then tried to get him to stand in a sauce pot for a photo op (he's a St. Bernard). Or the time I tried to go wineglass-for-wineglass with a high-tolerance Brit and ended up gracelessly stumbling off my barstool on the way to the bathroom. I'm sure a few guys went to the bar and recounted to their friends the awful first date they'd had the night before—with me.

Still, there were lots of men who proved on date one that they were far from Mr. Right. One told me my career aspirations were naive and that I'd be unemployed within the year. Another used a wheelchair but didn't seem concerned that I lived on a fourth-floor walk-up. One guy appeared promising until he announced midway through our chicken tikka masala that he'd just gotten a grain of rice stuck between his throat and his nasal passage, and then proceeded to emit a series of dreadful snorting sounds, I assume to dislodge it. It stuck around. Probably longer than I did.

These stories became my friends' favorite conversations. At dinner parties and weddings, I was often put on the spot with, "Tell them the one about the divorced guy who compared you to his ex-wife all night and then the restaurant to the hall where he got married!" My friends loved sharing their own dating disasters, and I heard stories that were embarrassing, awkward, and usually hysterical. We spent hours rehashing and analyzing not-great dates—what his weirdness meant, and whether he deserved a second chance or we should block him on Match.com.

I realized that single people want to hear every horrible first-date story because it's reassuring that it isn't just happening to one of us—it's part of the process for all single folk. Coupled-up people like hearing about bad dates too, probably because it makes them elated that they aren't still single. So whatever your romantic status, you probably like hearing about other people's mishaps. As it turns out, awful first dates may be awkward, shocking, or downright painful. But in the end, they're good material.

It seemed there was a whole community of women who wanted a place to bitch about dates gone wrong. So I made a website, www.awfulfirstdates.com, and posted a few of my stories. Then my friends started posting their stories, and within a few weeks, more than a thousand anecdotes poured in from all across the United States, England, Canada, and Australia. I decided to keep them anonymous so more people would be willing to share what they'd been through, and also not to incriminate the bad daters. The best—er, worst—of those stories, plus dozens of new ones, became the basis of this book. I've edited them, added a title for each, and then organized them into thematic categories based on the way things went wrong (the guy drank too much on the date, was weird about money, was actually married, etc.). Though there were a few stories that were tough to categorize or fit into multiple categories because the guy combined a slew of sleazy mistakes, it's shocking that there are basically only eleven different ways to screw up a first date.

In my career as a magazine writer, I often get the opportunity to chat with hot famous people. And unlike Cindy Crawford and Jennifer Lopez, I found that most of them have had the bad luck to go on a not-so-stellar first date. Hearing from some of the world's most successful and attractive actresses, musicians, and fashion designers that even they've experienced dating disasters is kind of inspiring, especially considering that many of them are now in happy relationships. Laughing with *Gossip Girl*'s Leighton Meester about a date she went on with a rich boy who was so spoiled he once got angry at his maid and reacted by throwing his laptop in his pool gives me hope; she is beautiful, talented, and successful, and yet still has to contend with the kind of guys who make you swear you wouldn't mind joining a nunnery. Or Salma Hayek, a talented multilingual producer, actress, and all-around gorgeous woman, who told me about a first date she went on…with the man who ended up becoming her husband and father to her child. That's the thing about bad dates: they happen to almost all of us. And though Hayek is part of the rare few for whom a bad date turns into a good relationship, even a painfully awful date can eventually make us laugh.

Awful First Date: Hollywood Dispatch

"I went out with an actor who said he'd come to see me in the play I was in and then we'd go out afterward for a drink or dinner. Then he called to downgrade it to nothing after, just him coming to my performance. He showed up at intermission."

—Kim Cattrall

Chapter 1

MR. MONOPOLY MONEY

n the movie *Kissing Jessica Stein*, Jessica is a single New Yorker who's set up on a first date with a nerdy accountant-type who can barely make conversation. When the check comes, he gets out a calculator and starts tabulating both shares of the bill: "We split the salad," he says, "but as I recall, you ate a little bit more, including more of the arugula, which is one of the more expensive greens. I didn't have any of the goat cheese; I'm allergic… You have exact change?"

It used to be so simple: the guy paid. Dinner, movie, whatever—on a first date, both parties knew that the check would automatically go to the man. (Of course, this system probably sucked for men, especially broke ones.) Then, along with female empowerment came female date confusion—who should pay? Even if you've had a great dinner, it inevitably makes for an awkward dance when the check comes. Should he pay, because that's the long-standing tradition? Should you offer to pay to show that you're an equal who values her independence and isn't just looking for a free meal? Should whoever asked for the date pay? Should you offer to split it, or does that show you don't like him? Will he feel like you owe him something if he pays?

It's also difficult to decide what's worse: a flashy guy who tries to overcompensate by throwing money around on a date, or a guy who can't afford to spot you a Starbucks. More often, women have to deal with broke-as-a-joke men, or at least ones who don't want to spend their money treating a date. Those may be the worst kind, where the guy clearly has money—he just isn't convinced you're worth spending it on, a fact he doesn't hide all that well.

It's not that the guy's financial situation is precisely the problem, or that you should start requiring a credit check before you agree to meet for drinks. I've certainly dated more than a few starving-artist types and had a great time. But the thing is, if they're not going to spend even ten bucks on your date, that's fine, but it means they need to be creative about planning an outing to a park or hitting a museum on free-admission day—some way to show you that if they weren't willing or able to spend money on the date, they spent time thinking about it and planning it. Instead, what many guys seem to do is to set up a traditional date, and then bust out a coupon or gift card, or do worse—like straight-up asking the woman to pay up.

Sure, Mr. Monopoly Money may eventually want to fall in love—but for tonight, he's just meeting up with you in hopes of a free dinner.

CALL HIM MONEYBAGS

After he asked me out, it took him over two months to finally arrange something, but fair enough: we're both busy people. He picked a fancy restaurant, and I thought over dinner we bonded well. When the bill came, I politely offered to pay half, which he accepted. But then he pulled out a 50 percent off coupon he'd printed out and told me, "This covers my half."

BIG SPENDER

He asked me out to dinner, then picked a fancy-schmancy restaurant. He ordered hors d'oeuvres, steak, champagne; I was impressed a grad student could afford such extravagances. When the bill came, he visibly jumped at the total. I'd only ever seen this reaction as a joke, but he was dead serious. Speechless, he slid the bill over to me to share his shock. Since it was hard to ignore the color draining from his face, I offered to split it. He thought about it for a while and concluded: "Well, um, well…no. No. You're…worth it? Yeah. You're worth it." It didn't sound like he was too convinced.

RECESSION BONUS

I was happy to see there was a really good-looking student sitting near me in one of my graduate classes, so I asked him out. He wanted to go to a bar, and I told him I don't drink…which he took as a sign that I needed to spend the rest of the night hearing the highlight reel of his various drunken escapades. One involved him paying for sex, and he boasted, "The price of prostitutes has been dropping because of the bad economy."

SPARE ANY CHANGE?

He was temping/freelancing, and I thought it was kind of admirable that he wasn't corporate. We made plans to grab dinner at a Mexican place. When we met up, he ordered a beer, and I got a margarita. We looked at the menu, and I asked what he was getting. He said, "Oh, I actually already ate, so I'm just having this beer." I was starving, so now I was forced to eat by myself in front of him, even though we had made plans to *eat dinner*. So I ate, and he watched me, looking hungry. The bill came and I said, "Just give me a few bucks for the beer, and I'll pay the rest." He proceeded to spill out a pile of pennies, nickels, and dimes all over the table, telling me he fished through the couch for change to pay for his big night out.

NO-BUCKS AT STARBUCKS

We made plans to go to a movie and then get coffee afterward. I offered to pay for the movie if he sprung for the coffee. We were supposed to meet at the movie theater, but he was twenty minutes late, so we missed the movie. I was pretty annoyed but tried to let it go as we walked to the coffee shop. As soon as I order my mocha, he pipes up, "Since you got out of paying for the movie, why don't you get the coffee?"

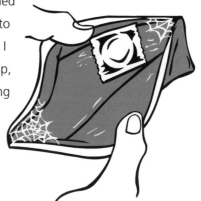

ONE PLATE, ONE GIFT CARD

When setting up our date, he repeated several times, "I'm going to pay for all this. I want it to be a *real* date." I pick him up, and we head to a Thai restaurant he picked in a seedy part of town. There are absolutely *no* customers except for us—strange for 7:30 p.m. on a Friday night. I have no idea why we drove all the way out here, seeing as there are a bunch of Thai restaurants closer in, but I soon realize why: he wants to have an art show in the gallery below the restaurant and didn't want to take the long bus ride to check it out, so he figured he'd just tack the visit on to the date. As we look at the menu, he comments about how expensive everything is—he orders a water and asks if we can share something (I again offer to go dutch, but he's still adamant about paying). We get our food, and when the server doesn't bring me a plate, I ask for one, to which my date says, "Let's just use one." I thought it was to be romantic, but it was actually so he could eat almost the entire thing himself. We head to the movies, where he complains about the price of tickets, the price of popcorn, the price of soda…and pays for the whole thing with a gift card he got for his birthday a few years ago! I gladly dropped him off after the movie and didn't return his text the next day that said, "Next time it's your turn."

CREDIT CARDS ARE BAD...AND SO IS HE

This guy asked me out to dinner, and we had great conversation, great beer, great food. Then the waitress drops off the check, and it sits at the table for probably ten minutes and he hasn't offered to pay, so I figure we're splitting it, which is fine. So I put down my half and hand the check to him. That's when he says he doesn't have any money (in our conversation, he'd mentioned he has two jobs). I say, "You're seriously doing this? That's a pretty ballsy move." He tells me, "Credit cards are evil." I ask if he has any cash then. He says no, and to prove this, he takes his wallet out of his pocket, counts out $23 in cash, says, "See? I don't have any money," and *puts the cash back* in his wallet.

DOLLAR DOLLAR BILLS, Y'ALL

He picked me up in an iridescent convertible and made sure to rev the engine a few times before coming to my door. On the way to the movie theater, he revved the engine at every red light, which was mortifying. He apologized, but not for that, saying, "Oh sorry, my eyebrows look a bit unruly. I didn't have them waxed this week." Then he paid for our tickets with a $100 bill because "that's the only bill worth carrying."

IT'S ALL IN THE JEANS

We went to a movie theater where you eat and watch a movie at the same time. When my date tried to pay, his card was declined, and neither of us had any cash. Since my date had been drinking, I had to miss the last fifteen minutes of the movie to drive *his* car to the closest ATM to get cash. Later, he admitted to a mutual friend that he'd maxed out his credit card buying designer jeans that morning.

SHORT AND (NOT) SWEET

Two friends had set me up with a very wealthy investment banker, who was about a foot shorter than me. I probably could've gotten over it, but he kept making cracks about how tall I was and calling me "an Amazon woman." When I said I needed to get home, he insisted on driving me to my car (he'd done valet, while I had self-parked in the massive garage), which seemed like an excuse to show off his Lexus SUV. I honestly couldn't remember where my car was, but he took my confusion as an act intended to get more time with him and kept trying to put his hand on my knee. Sitting in a humongous SUV has never felt so constricting—when I saw my car, I practically jumped out of his while it was still moving.

HEY, BIG SPENDER

When the bill came, he asked if we could split it. I had a $10 salad and water, while he'd had the lamb and several drinks. The restaurant didn't accept my credit card, so I had to leave the table to find an ATM. When I returned with the cash and rolled my eyes, he justified it by saying, "Well, I'm never going to see you again."

MODERN FAMILY

I was on a blind date with a high-school teacher. I asked him what his career goals were, and he said, "I hope to retire in ten years." I'm thinking that being able to retire at forty would be pretty impressive on a public-school teacher's salary. So I say, "That's great you've been saving up to retire early. Good for you!" To which he replied, "Nah, my parents are old, and *they're* loaded. I'm just waiting for them to kick it, so I inherit all that cash and don't have to work anymore."

DRUNK AND BROKE

We met at a lovely Italian restaurant, where he proceeded to drink a bottle of wine by himself and make awkward conversation about video games and his old frat brothers. When the check came, he said he was short on cash, and he couldn't cover his half. It was the end of the month, he said, and he'd already spent his paycheck on rent, beer, and pay-per-view boxing matches.

Awful First Dates: Hollywood Dispatch

"I made a picnic up on a mountain for a girl, with tables and chairs and three courses. It took me a full day to carry it all up there. But then she never showed, and the wind and rain blew in. The whole night was a washout."

—Bear Grylls, host of *Man vs. Wild*

Chapter 2

MR. "IT'S FIVE O'CLOCK SOMEWHERE"

We get it. Meeting a new person and potentially getting a chance to make out with him is high-stakes, nervous-making stuff. After all, Jerry Seinfeld once described a date as "pressure and tension. What is a date, really, but a job interview that lasts all night? The only difference between a date and a job interview is that in not many job interviews is there a chance you'll end up naked at the end of it." Everyone knows that for a date, just as for a job interview, you should show up highlighting your best self: looking good, smelling good, and most certainly not already drunk. But there's obviously a reason alcohol is nicknamed liquid courage—it can make you feel less self-conscious, less nervous, and a lot more confident and sexy (even though you'll actually come off as the exact opposite with a third margarita dribbling down your chin).

Drinking greases the wheels of a first date, easing conversation and helping you be a little less aware of the fact that your every move may be evaluated and judged. After all, sharing a bottle of wine over dinner or ordering a few drinks at a bar while you get to know each other is practically a first-date ritual. It's delicious, calming, and fun—and you can tell a lot about your date by whether he orders a fruity drink full of fruit garnishes and umbrellas, whatever beer's on tap, or a Four Loko.

The downside is when you drink too much on a date, since there's really no hangover as strong as waking up with his name tattooed on your ass. Or when your date drinks too much, to the point where in a moment he swerves from "fun and tipsy" to "starting a bar fight with a biker gang." Or when he gets so drunk that he then calls you by the wrong name. Or asks you to bail him out of jail. Or page his AA sponsor. Or even worse—when he throws up on your new shoes.

SOMEBODY CALL AA

My date immediately asked our waiter for two shots of tequila and a beer. I said, "Oh, thanks, but I don't really take shots," but he explained they were both for him. He slammed them and asked for another one, "to sip at." Forty-five minutes later, he'd "sipped" another three shots and a steady stream of beers. Then, when I said I needed to head home, he offered to *drive* me.

VOMITRON

We met at a bar, and after a few hours of heavy drinking, he came home with me. We started to make out, and he called me "Melissa"—not even close to my name. Then he stood up and ran to the bathroom but didn't make it, projectile vomiting all over the hallway and into my closet and shoes (with my orthotics in them). When I went to clean it up, he tried to undress me, and I pushed him away (the smell of vomit is not really a turn-on). So he then passed out in my bed, woke up after he had peed all over my sheets, and snuck out. Luckily, he left his cell phone by accident, which I used to call his friends and tell them what he'd done.

OFF THE WAGON

In our first conversation, he mentioned he didn't drink alcohol (fine with me). We made a date to go to the race track, and when we met there, he was holding a six-pack. Within fifteen minutes, he had already drained four bottles. We ran into his friend at the track, and they proceeded to have a drinking contest of chugging rum and Cokes. He was so blitzed that I decided to just leave and catch a train home myself. As he walked me to the train station, he stopped to urinate on a car; then, as I went to get on the train, he started to wail that if I actually tried to leave, he would throw himself on the track (I left anyway). I got a call from him five hours later…because he was in jail for public intoxication and wanted me to come bail him out.

DR. PUSHOVER

On the phone, he'd said he wasn't really a drinker. But while I had two glasses of wine at dinner, he knocked back four red wines and four more glasses of Johnny Walker on the rocks. Um, not a drinker? Okay, maybe he was nervous. As he stumbled to the door and asked me to do things to him I wouldn't do on a first date (and probably not *ever*), I commented that for a nondrinker, he certainly seemed to drink quite a bit. He got really angry and yelled, "I was only drinking because you were and you seemed to expect me to!" Peer pressure is for high-school kids. The weirdest part is that he works as a doctor in a rehab center.

NO FRIGGIN' PROBLEM HERE

When we meet up to go to a hockey game, he smells like booze and reveals he has chugged a six-pack because "the beers in the arena are so expensive." He is drunk and won't shut up. At the game, I'm thirsty and mention I'd like a beer. [crickets] Since he doesn't offer, I say I'll get myself one and him one ($8 a pop, he has a point), and he says

"Oh yeah, that'd be great!" He gets drunker and won't shut up. I learn intimate details of ex-girlfriends and his grandmother's incontinence. He also regales me with a tale of a work event where he got "a bit tipsy" and was told to leave, because he may have a drinking problem. He informs me, in breath laden with Bud Light, "I don't have a friggin' problem. I'm a friggin' young guy. I just friggin' like to have friggin' fun."

A REAL CATCH

I met a guy online, and we had a great dinner. But as the night progressed, he kept drinking to the point of becoming obnoxious. When I drove him home, he insisted on smoking a cigar in my car and farted loudly several times, laughing hysterically. I obviously didn't contact him and didn't hear from him either, until a week later, when he texted me that he was getting back together with his ex, but would still be interested in hooking up if things didn't work out with her.

NO SEX, ON THE BEACH OR ELSEWHERE

We met at a Mexican restaurant because I like to celebrate Cinco de Mayo. I ordered a Corona, and he ordered a Sex on the Beach. Seriously. The bartender said he didn't know how to make a Sex on the Beach, and pointed out that this was a Mexican restaurant that specialized in margaritas, but the guy wouldn't quit. "But you have a bottle of vodka right there," he said. "You just add cranberry juice and orange juice to that." He was basically throwing a hissy fit. The bartender apologized and said that they didn't have cranberry juice or orange juice, and would he like a beer. My date then said he would go to the drugstore next door and buy Ocean Spray juices if the bartender would mix it for him. I had no idea why he was so fixated on this particular drink, but while he went to the store, I snuck out and ran the other direction.

SAFETY FIRST

I had been talking to this guy online for a while, and he seemed really into me. I was spending the weekend house-sitting for a friend who lived near him, so I suggested that we meet up for coffee or a drink, but told him that first I had to run back to my place to get something I'd forgotten. He offered to pick me up and take me there, which I thought was nice of him. On the drive there, he was weaving in and out of his lane and speeding, and when I made a nervous comment, he confessed that he'd had a "few beers" before he arrived. By the time we got back, the coffee shop we'd intended on going to was closed, so I suggested that we go instead to the restaurant/bar across the street. He then said, "You have a way home, right? Because I'm going to want to drink more and I'll be taking a cab." At this point, I said that perhaps he should just drop me off. He did, and then was upset that I wouldn't invite him up or give him a kiss good night.

CAN'T YOU HEAR
ME CALLING?

I went out with a guy who seemed fun and cute. He drank three glasses of whiskey in the first hour (I gave up on keeping up with him after the second one) and went on to tell me a story about drunk-dialing his ex. "I think a girl should be flattered when she's drunk-dialed," he said. "It's like, 'Look, I'm drunk and I'm thinking about being with *you*.'" I thought that was weird, but we also didn't have great chemistry, so I didn't mind when we parted ways early. Later that night I woke up to my phone ringing—guess who was drunk-dialing me at 2 a.m.?

REDHEADS HAVE MORE FUN

We met online and arranged to meet at a bar. I waited for thirty minutes, only for him to show up drunk. Not tipsy, but dump-his-martini-all-over-me-in-the-first-five-minutes drunk. He then kept grabbing at me and told me close to forty times that he liked redheads, while petting my hair. When I went to leave, he proceeded to tell the bartender, the host, and anyone on the street—as I ran to catch a cab—that I was a bitch for bailing on him. Then several months later, I was out for my birthday with my sister (she's also a redhead). She points out this guy who she'd briefly dated but ultimately turned out to be a jerk (I had heard the horror stories and never knew who the mystery idiot was) and, of course, it was the *same guy*.

GETTING THEIR MONEY'S WORTH

I met a guy online and decided to meet up for dinner (which I would buy) and drinks (which he would buy). He was an hour and a half late, but he kept calling to let me know he was on his way. When he showed up, he looked nothing like the picture he sent me…and eventually revealed that the picture was over *seven years old*, from when he was 100 *pounds* lighter. Foolishly, I decided to give him the benefit of the doubt and stick it out.

He picked the most expensive restaurant on the street, since I was paying. I ordered a $13 main dish and a glass of wine. He ordered a $28 seafood platter and a *bottle* of wine. After mediocre conversation, I decided to leave, but then had a better idea: I needed to even things out by getting absolutely plastered on his dime. So we went to a bar where I proceeded to order the most expensive martinis on the menu. Before long I was hammered. Unfortunately, my genius plan backfired because I ended up taking him home for the worst one-night stand in history.

SID IN SEARCH OF HIS NANCY

I drive to his place to pick him up for a movie, and it turns out to be a tiny trailer in the middle of nowhere. He suggests we stay in and watch his favorite movie, a documentary about G. G. Allin, some punk-rock singer who used to cut himself onstage and roll in poop (and sometimes eat it). While we were watching, my date got drunk and raved about how he's just like G. G. Allin and why he's his idol. He also kept offering to pull out his ouija board. Once he passed out, I nudged him to say I was leaving. I was halfway home when the guy starts sending me angry texts, saying I was so rude for leaving. I hope he and the ghost of G. G. are very happy together.

A DIFFERENT KIND OF EXCESSIVE DRINKING

We went out to dinner one night in August. He was sweating despite the air conditioning, and he immediately asked the waiter to bring over water, which he gulped down in seconds. (I figured he was hot because it was, you know, August.) But he just kept drinking—he needed his glass refilled six times before our food even arrived; after that, I lost count. He was super twitchy, which I first thought was nerves. But as he went to the bathroom three times during dinner (and came back more jittery each time), I started to think he wasn't dehydrated—he was on coke.

DÉJÀ VU

At my favorite bar, I kept catching this guy looking at me. Finally one night he introduced himself. Then he said, "I'm not interested in playing games. I just want to get to know a pretty girl—is that so wrong?" He came across as super sweet and earnest, if a little tipsy—he said drinking helped with his shyness. It was super flattering, because he really seemed excited about going out with me. But then a week went by, and he never called. I figured we'd just catch each other at the bar. And we did. He hobbled over, blitzed out of his mind, and reintroduced himself with the same damn speech.

RED RED WINE, MAKE ME FEEL SO FINE

I'd agreed to meet my date for an early drink at a wine bar, but when he got there it was clear that he'd already hit up a few happy hours on his own. He stumbled past me twice before he recognized me, teetered on his bar stool, and then ordered some pasta to help him sober up. I was impressed that he managed not to spill too much marinara on himself, but not enough to ever call him again.

Awful First Dates: Hollywood Dispatch

"I've been on a lot more bad first dates than good ones—there's been so many. For one, my mother set me up, which should have been a red flag. He and I didn't talk for the majority of the date—we just sat there in awkward silence. I ate as quickly as I could to speed up getting out of there."

—Lauren Conrad

Chapter 3

MR. SEXUAL SUPER-FREAK

After a great first date, it's perfectly welcome for a guy to go in for a good-night kiss...but it's never okay for him to go for the good-night leg hump. Maybe he's overly aggressive, or maybe he's just clueless, but either way, there are few things that have you reaching for Mace faster than a guy who gets too grabby too quickly. There are a surprising number of stories, too, of men who know there's zero chemistry and try to take you home regardless. It may seem ridiculous for them to try to score when a date is going so poorly, but it's actually a totally logical Hail Mary play: the guy has nothing else to lose. Since you already don't like him, maybe if he comes on strong you'll offer him some pity-makeout, and worst comes to worst, you'll just leave, which he was planning on happening anyway. Still, the audacity is impressive (and gross).

Or maybe you were into him and sending him the green light, but his moves just didn't do it for you. After all, to one woman, a man who baby-talks might be superhot sexual kryptonite; to another, it's "Oh my God, did he just ask for a 'widdle kissy-wissy'?" And if a move worked for a guy once, he's likely to keep trying it on every woman he takes out…which means the one woman who encouraged baby-talk—or eyeball-licking, or a sex swing—may be the reason your first date is trying it out on you. But there are also stories of moves that are so hideously bad (coming in for a first kiss with your mouth full of deviled eggs? Really, dude?) that we can't believe they worked on anyone, ever.

Then there are the cases of showing his kinkiness too soon. In the context of a happy, healthy relationship, full of trust and commitment, the average woman would probably be into, or at least willing to try, experimenting with some nonvanilla sex moves. But there may be no bigger turn-off than a guy trying to masturbate in front of you, drink your pee, or handcuff you to his van before you even know his middle name. But assuming you didn't meet by responding to a Craigslist fetish posting, it can make you wonder, if this is his *first date* move, how much further freakiness lies ahead? We all have our freak flags—but it wouldn't hurt these guys to fly theirs at half-mast for a few more dates.

SOLO ACT

We immediately hit it off—he was funny, intelligent, and fairly cute. After dinner, we began kissing in his living room. When he tried to take it further, I made it clear that I wasn't ready. In response, he immediately unzipped his pants, whipped it out, and began furiously masturbating in front of me.

EAT ME

I met a guy in Australia who was a good-looking surfer type. We went out for dinner, and over appetizers, he leaned across the table and reached toward my face. I thought he was going to stroke it (which would have been too intense anyway), but instead he pulled some sleep out of the corner of my eye, licked his finger, and said, "I can't wait to consume you."

AND NOW, FOR DESSERT

I went out with a guy for dinner, and we were having a pleasant chat about very general, superficial topics. About thirty minutes in, he paused, took a sip of wine, and then said, "So, can we go have sex now?" I looked at him, put on my coat, and left.

THE JELLY MAN

After hitting it off over dinner and drinks, we went back to his place and started some innocent kissing on the couch. After a few minutes, he got up and said he had to go to the restroom. When he came out and sat back down on the couch, I saw he'd brought with him a tube of KY.

THE SUBWAY HUMPER

After a great date, we decided to get on the subway home together, since we live in the same direction. I was even kind of excited when he kissed me in the middle of the crowded train. But then he grabbed my ass, jammed his hand into my back pocket, and gyrated awkwardly against my knee. He stuck his tongue in my ear, moaned loudly, and said, "Oh baby. You've got me all fired up." Ew.

AMERICAN GIGOLO

I found out at the end of the date that he was a prostitute.

WORTH A TRY

I met a cute guy at a convention, and we agreed to meet up the next night, since there was supposed to be a big party. But when I texted him to make plans, he said he wanted to hang out, but wasn't sure we should go to that party. I asked what he wanted to do instead, and he responded: "Well, there's a party in my pants…"

BUT IS HE A MAC OR A PC?

After a nice dinner and some drinks, I mentioned to him that I was having problems with my computer. My date, who was a computer science major, told me he could fix it, so I invited him back to my apartment. He seemed like a great guy and I was interested, although I'm not a hookup-on-the-first-date kinda gal.

I left him in the living room to get us some coffee. A couple of minutes later, I heard my roommate scream. She had walked in and found him standing in the middle of the room, completely naked. He said he'd heard that this move works one-third of the time and figured it was worth a try. I asked him to please leave. Instead, he sat down (still naked!) in my desk chair and continued to work on the computer. He didn't leave until I called the police, who arrived and asked him to put on some pants before they escorted him out.

GETTING HANDSY

He was super boring to talk to, but it was a harmless enough evening. But when he was driving me back to my place, he offered up that he had a hand fetish and proceeded to rub my hand in a creepy manner all the way home. Then, when we got to my door, instead of kissing me on the mouth, he reached for my hand and kissed it, which was kind of weird but also polite…until he started tonguing between my fingers and I had to yank it away from him and go inside.

DINNER 'N' HUMP

After buying me a Subway sandwich for dinner and then saying, "Don't say I never bought you anything," he told me he had to run an errand to his grandparents' house, where he tried to get me to have sex with him on the washing machine in their basement.

HE'S A HOOVER

After a wonderful date, he walked me to my door—very gentlemanly—and asked for a goodnight kiss. After I gave him the green light, I felt this crazy pressure on my lips, like he was trying to suck them into his mouth, so I pulled away. First kisses are always awkward…so I gave it another shot. Again, he started sucking on my lips and after about thirty seconds, the pain became unbearable, so I said good night. The next day, my mouth was covered in deep purple hickies that hurt too much to try to cover with lipstick.

THE VAN MAN

I'd been talking to a man online for a couple months and agreed to have dinner with him. Turns out, instead of being in his early thirties as he'd claimed, he was clearly closer to fifty. We had strained conversation over dinner, mainly talking about how he didn't want to live with his mother anymore. As we walked out, he told me he wanted to show me his new wheels: a shiny, black conversion van, aka a kidnapper-mobile. He then asked if I wanted to go for a ride and opened the side door. Inside was a sex swing and handcuffs attached to the ceiling! I ran back inside the restaurant and had a waiter walk me to my car.

OH SNAP!

We went out bowling, and we were having a good time. For our second game, we decided to make up funny names for each other in the computer. While I was sitting in the chair typing, he came up behind me and, over my shirt, started fumbling around the middle of my back. I started flailing around and yelping—I thought there must have been a bug or something on my back he was trying to get off me. He said there wasn't and he stopped, but a few minutes later I felt him grabbing at my back again—I asked him what the hell he was doing, and he proudly admitted he was trying to show me his skills at unhooking a bra!

IF THAT'S WHAT YOU'RE INTO

I'd been warned before going to see the movie *Irreversible* that it included some graphic sex scenes, but my date and I joked that we could handle it. Turns out, I couldn't: it was a horribly depressing story that ends with a crazy-intense, nearly ten-minute long street-rape scene. It was so gnarly that people were sobbing and walking out of the theater; I thought I was going to faint. But apparently the scene had the opposite effect on my date, because the moment we got out of the theater, he was all over me.

TOUCHY-FEELY

I knew a guy who told all our friends that he really liked me, but I didn't find him attractive at all. He kept asking me out and I always made excuses; one time, to be nice, I finally agreed to go to the movies with him. At one point during the film, he started stroking my knee; I moved it away. I guess he realized I had a hole in the knee of my jeans, because a few minutes later, I thought there was a worm in my pants—it was actually my date, who had shoved his fingers inside the hole and was basically fingering my leg.

THE OCTOPUS

He picks me up and says we're going to his friend's bar. When we get there, it's in the middle of nowhere in a shipping area for freight trucks, completely surrounded by giant deserted warehouses. We go into the bar, and we're the only people there besides his friend, the bartender. My date does shots all night and starts eating those nasty pickled eggs and sausages out of the jar behind the bar. I ask him to take me home, and he grabs me and starts open-mouth kissing my *face*, covering it with pickled-egg and sausage slobber as he grabs my breasts and butt and chants, "Spend the night! Spend the night!"

THE NO-CUDDLE ZONE

He was a dark, handsome grad student, and we bonded quickly over our mutual appreciation of sci-fi and craft beer. So I didn't regret going home with him...until I woke up in the middle of the night and he'd disappeared from his own apartment. I called his cell phone in a panic, and he explained, "I don't like to cuddle, so I'm staying at my office overnight. You can let yourself out in the morning."

IN A PINCH

We went back to his house and started kissing. Then we were just lying in bed enjoying pillow talk when he started randomly pinching the skin of my elbow and twisting it—hard. I asked what he was doing and he said he had always done that to whomever he shared his bed with, and then gave the example, "You know, like my mom and my sisters."

THE NAKED TRUTH

We hit it off, so I said I'd watch a movie at his apartment. A few minutes into it, I realized I was not interested in him and just wanted to go home. After his numerous attempts to try to kiss me (and me telling him it wasn't going to happen), I asked if he could take me home. He said he was too drunk to drive and that I should just spend the night. I may have considered sleeping on a couch, but his apartment was a studio, so that wasn't an option. He informed me that he sleeps naked; then he stripped down and hopped into bed. I walked out and called a cab.

THIRSTY THURSDAY

I had dinner and great conversation with a man I met online. In front of my apartment, I thanked him again for treating me to dinner, and he asked if he could kiss me good night. I said yes and we had a hot first kiss. Then he paused to ask if I would be willing to urinate in a glass so he could drink it. I guess I'll have to think about that—from the other side of my locked apartment door!

SMOOTH SEXTER

He picked me up to go to the movies and proceeded to chain-smoke cigarettes and spit out the window. Then he spent the whole movie trying to kiss me and cuddle (I managed to avoid all of his advances). After the movie, he asked me to dinner (I said no) then asked me out for the following night (I also said no). Finally, I got him to drop me off at my apartment. A few minutes later I got a couple calls from him that I ignored. This was followed by a text saying "SEX?"

MR. SANDMAN

After a fun date, we started making out. I was really into it and started kissing his stomach…and then I looked up and realized he had fallen asleep.

MODESTY LOST

I started talking with him online, and when we met in person, I realized he looked a little familiar, so I asked if he recognized me too. Yes, he informed me—I had dated his roommate. As if that wasn't awkward enough, my date then told me that though the roommate had never formally even introduced us, my date had already seen me naked. He then said that my ex, unbeknownst to me, had a habit of leaving his door wide open after I'd gone to bed, not caring that both of his roommates would see me sleeping naked.

A STRAIGHT SHOOTER

I went on a first date with a cop who I'd met in a bar. We went out to dinner, and although he wasn't in uniform, he was still wearing his gun. I told myself it was no big deal; he was nice and funny, and I figured maybe he was required to wear it at all times for work or something. As he started having more drinks, he told me that actually, he specifically strapped the gun on for our date. He also told me that he wasn't supposed to be wearing his gun at all while he was drinking, but he just liked it. As he got pro-gressively drunker, he kept asking me if I wanted to touch his gun. I politely declined, but he was insistent. Eventually, he grabbed my hand, put it on his gun, and held it there, purring, "Mmm…how do you like it?"

IT'S IN HIS KISS

We went out for coffee, and he insisted we stay and order food. I took my first bite, a huge mouthful of bruschetta; that's when he chose to lean over and give me a big open-mouth kiss. I said something like "'BLLLERRRRCHHHHH!"' and pushed him away. We finished up and he walked me to the train station. He goes, "Let's continue what we started earlier." Totally confused, I said, "What?" and as I had my mouth open, he came at my face again, tongue out.

WITH FRIENDS LIKE THESE

My ex dumped me and I was heartbroken. A few weeks later, when he was out of town, I went out with his group of friends, including the mutual friend who originally introduced us. The guy was being very complimentary all evening and I was starting to remember what it was like to flirt. We kissed at the end of the night and I thought maybe I'd been dating the wrong friend all along. Then he tried to push my head down and said, "Oh come on, just go down on me…[ex's name] says you're good!"

THE RUNAWAY

I met up with this guy at a bar, where we were having a great talk. We ran into a couple I'm friends with, so they came and sat with us for a while. Suddenly my date announced he had to go buy cigarettes. Instead of going to the grocery store across the street from the bar, out the big front window we could see him cross the parking lot in the other direction, get in his car, and drive away. A few minutes later I received a text message from him asking me where I was. I answered, "Uh, still sitting in the bar where you just ditched me." He then texted back, "I'll pick you up and we can go have sex." Needless to say, I didn't respond and my friends laughed about it all night.

MASTER OF HER DOMAIN

We went back to my apartment and started making out. We were still fully clothed when he suddenly asked me if I would masturbate in front of him.

Awful First Dates: Hollywood Dispatch

"I was out walking around with a woman on our first date, and she ran into two of her friends. While she was turned around to talk to them, a bird shit on me. I have a horrible gag reflex, so I knew that if I didn't get away from it I would vomit. So I ripped my shirt off and then she turned around to introduce me, and I was standing there shirtless, to them for no reason, like 'Hey, I'm Justin.'"

—Justin Halpern, author of *Sh*t My Dad Says*

Chapter 4
MR. NOT-QUITE-SINGLE

There's an old saying about how men are just like parking spots: all the good ones are taken. To take that analogy a step further, the women in this chapter were cruising around the mall parking lots at Christmastime—crowded with competition and no spots in sight. They thought they'd have to park in Lot Y, several time zones away, or keep circling the rows all night in vain. Then their eyes landed on an open space, and a glorious one at that, one right near the Nordstrom entrance! It seemed they'd finally lucked out. Woo hoo! But as they go to maneuver into the spot, they stop short, inches from hitting the bumper of another car already parked there—a tiny Mini Cooper that was hidden from view. That Mini Cooper is the girlfriend or—even worse, wife—these daters didn't quite anticipate.

It would be easy to hate the "other woman"—but in these cases, the woman didn't know she was the other woman until she was already on the date. *Sigh*. If only men had to wear engagement rings. Or, you know, didn't troll online dating sites when they're already in a relationship. Or admitted they were married before their tongue was in your mouth. Sure, a lot of the good ones are taken—but a lot of the taken ones aren't good.

PUT A RING ON IT

When I was in college, I went on a fabulous date with a grad student, and we were clearly totally into each other. On the way home, he parked his car outside my dorm and leaned across to kiss me good night. Before we could make contact, his phone rang. Much to my chagrin, he answered. "Hello? Oh hi, honey. We're out of what? Tomatoes? Sure, I'll pick some up on my way home." When I asked who it was, he told me it was his fiancée. And then leaned in again.

BI-CURIOUS

I had my eye on this guy for a long time, and I was *so* happy when he finally asked me out. He took me to a romantic restaurant, and I thought the date went well. Afterward we were making out in his car outside my apartment when he said that it had been fun, and he knew that I liked him, but he wouldn't be asking me out again…because he had a big crush on this Chinese guy at his office.

WHICH ONE OF US IS HE ON A DATE WITH?

He showed up half an hour late to pick me up for dinner, and then apologized for the smell of the car as he'd come "straight from the gym." Once he picked a restaurant, he kept flirting with the waitress, like comparing notes with her on their mutually shaved arms (he said his was for swimming…sure). It turns out he'd been out with her a few times, and it seemed he'd only brought me there to make her jealous. He hardly bothered talking to me at all and actually pulled up a chair for her so she could join us. I just sat there while they talked, feeling like I was the odd man out on their date.

FRIENDS WITH BENEFITS

Over drinks, he tells me he has a four-year-old son who lives out of state.

"With his mother?" I say.

"Yeah, with my wife," he says.

"You mean ex-wife?"

"Technically, I'm still married," he says. "We stay married for the benefits."

"Oh, the health benefits?"

"Among others."

GREAT EX-PECTATIONS

He spent the whole date obsessively talking about his ex-wife, even saying, "She's an absolutely stunning woman." He said he'd get over her, though, because all his female coworkers, his best friend, and even his own *cousin* were attracted to him. I never heard from him again, until a mutual friend said the guy didn't call because I clearly wasn't over my ex. Um, pot, kettle, black!

SPIN CYCLE SHENANIGANS

A guy I'd liked finally asked if he could come over and watch a movie. He arrived at my house that evening with Prince's *Purple Rain* as well as a hardcore porn DVD...and a load of laundry. He told me we could watch the movies while he did some laundry and popped in *Purple Rain* (at least he started with the movie and not the porn) and asked if I had any quarters he could "borrow." Because I'm an idiot, I figured doing chores together would mean we were that much closer to being a real couple, and I gladly forked over ten quarters and helped him put a load into the washer. We snuggled up together on my couch to watch the movie and started making out. Mid-kiss, he yelled into my mouth, "I have a girlfriend!" I pushed him away, stunned. He told me they were living together and that he'd gotten out for the night by telling her he was going to the Laundromat. The only thing that could make this night better was that his clothes still had twenty minutes left in the dryer, so we sat awkwardly next to each other watching the movie until his laundry was done.

SHE CAN KEEP HIM

He took me out to this nice Japanese restaurant, where we talked about family and life. After that we went shopping at a few stores, and I bought a DVD. He suggested we go back to his place to watch it, but I told him I'm not the kind of girl who goes to someone's house on a first date. He kept persisting, and I said no again. Eventually, he drove back to his apartment anyway, and I told him it was weird and I wouldn't go inside. He agreed to drive me home, and we made out a little in the car. That's when he brought up his ex-girlfriend and said, "Yeah, we're on a break right now. You're just a casual date, because we'll probably get back together next week."

COKE ZERO

He was a singer who'd just started to hit the big time. He gave me a backstage pass to his next show, where he proceeded to ask me to drive him to his drug dealer's house to buy cocaine, to a cooking-supplies store so he could buy whipped cream canisters for doing whippets, and to the after-party. He tried to kiss me on the highway while I was driving, and finally, he asked me to drive him to the train station so he could meet up with his *girlfriend and their new baby*. I dropped him off and didn't really think of him again until a few weeks later—when I moved the passenger seat of my car and found the huge bag of coke he'd accidentally left there.

SOMETHING'S FISHY

He invited me to dinner on his roof deck and grilled me a piece of tuna. It was not only the largest piece of fish I'd ever seen (I'd told him I was a vegetarian, and I guess he thought that meant I eat fish, which I don't)—it was also the toughest. But because he was a day laborer and didn't have much money, and I could tell he'd tried to impress me by getting an expensive piece of fish, I choked it down with a smile and finished the whole thing, trying not to gag the entire time. When I was done, he gently touched my arm and started telling me all about his girlfriend.

THE NETWORKER

An extremely handsome guy approached me at church and started flirting. We talked about work, and I mentioned that I owned a web development company. He asked for my card, smiled, and asked me to lunch. I hadn't been on a date since my divorce, so I was really excited. I called my friends, and they were really happy for me.

We planned the date for Friday after work at an upscale

sushi restaurant. When I arrived, I saw him…with a really pretty blonde. He introduced me to his long-distance girlfriend, who surprised him that day by arriving from another state. They spent the entire meal recounting how they met and how in love they were. I figured I'd totally misread him and maybe he was interested in web developing and just trying to network. But when she went to the bathroom, he started flirting with me again!

REUNITED AND IT FEELS SO…WEIRD

I had an amazing vacation romance with a friend of a friend, but we lived far away, and I decided it was better not to keep in touch. Still, I thought about him all the time. A year later, I heard from mutual friends that he was living near me, so I decided to tag along with them and surprise him to have the real first date we never got. When I saw him, he seemed overjoyed and spent the entire day glued to my side. We ended up going back to his room to have sex, which is when I saw his walls were plastered with pictures of his new girlfriend.

THE FAMILY MAN

We were having a great time at cocktails so decided to stay for dinner. We ordered a nice bottle of wine, and then his phone rang; he said he had to check in and would be back in five minutes. When he got back, I said, "Everything at work okay?" He corrected me—he was actually checking in to say good night to his fifteen-month-old daughter and his wife. I considered storming out or flipping the table...but I decided to order the lobster and the most expensive bottle of wine—and *then* walk out.

THE MESSAGE IS IN THE MASSAGE

I met a guy at a dance club, and I thought we really clicked—he had seen the same obscure films I like, and we made each other laugh. At the end of the evening, he gave me his card—he was a professional masseur—and, winking, said I should come by for a "free massage." I made the appointment for a week later. When I showed up, he not only told me about his live-in girlfriend, he charged me the full price.

Awful First Dates: Hollywood Dispatch

How to Avoid an Awful First Date: "I moved to the U.S. at 18 to model, and I thought going out with a stranger alone was a strange concept, so I would always bring along a friend on my first dates! No man ever complained about it, though, because the friend I'd bring along would always be another model."

—Iman

Chapter 5

MR. FASCIST

Racism, sexism, homophobia, and anti-Semitism should be relics of the past. If that's too much to ask, they at least shouldn't be busted out on the first date. It doesn't seem like women are asking for too much for a guy who doesn't judge people based on their race, sex, sexual orientation, nationality, or religion. I mean, if dating is the search for love, which is supposed to be the opposite of hate, why would you want to be with someone who breaks out the hate right off the bat?

A recent survey of 720,000 eHarmony members looked at men's and women's lists of "can't stands" in a partner, the things that would be nonnegotiable deal-breakers for a relationship. The ten most popular responses from men and women were pretty similar, with both sexes saying they aren't fans of lying, infidelity, laziness, bad hygiene, rude behavior, or using drugs. There was only one category that was completely different. The women also cited racism, saying, "I can't stand someone who believes that any ethnic group to which they belong is superior to the rest of humanity." The men, however, didn't vote racism into their top ten deal-breakers, instead opting for something that would make Martin Luther King Jr. just as proud: "I can't stand someone who is overweight."

With that, it should be no surprise that these guys aren't ashamed to be drinking Haterade on their first dates—yet somehow it still is.

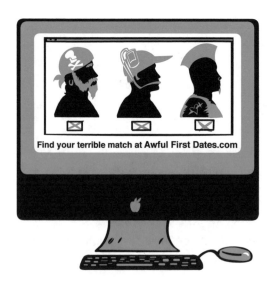

Find your terrible match at Awful First Dates.com

THE DRIVING NAZI

On our way from dinner to a movie, a car whipped out of a parking lot, cutting us off. He screamed at the car, "F-ing Jew!" I was obviously taken aback and asked him what the driver's religion had to do with his driving skills. This started him on a ten-minute monologue about how the gays and the blacks and the Jews (although he used slurs in place of the words "gay" and "black") were destroying America. Instead of going to the movie, I asked to be dropped off at home. Two weeks later, he left me a message saying, "I'm sorry. I didn't mean to insult your people."

ISO: DIVERSITY TRAINING

I went on a date with my coworker, who's a sweet-but-dorky white guy. In mid-conversation, he dropped the N-word like it was nothing. I didn't know if I should tell him that even though I look light-skinned, I'm actually half black.

WOMAN-HATER

The waitress gave me a weird look when she brought me to where my blind date was waiting. He was on his second martini, and downed it and ordered another before I could get my first drink. From the moment I sat down to the moment I left (fifteen excruciating minutes), he spewed venom about his ex-wife, and then decided everything he said about her applied to *all* women. As I got up to leave, he slurred, "So I hate women…does that mean you have be such a bitch and leave?"

HE'S NOT THE CAT'S MEOW

We had only a so-so dinner, and on the drive back, a cat darts in front of the car and we hit it. I start crying and tell him we need to stop and check on the cat and possibly take it to a vet, and he starts telling me that like "all women," I'm a "total pussy."

HANUKKAH HARRY

Last December, I met a guy out for drinks, and the bar had a small Christmas tree and some decorations up. (I happen to be Jewish but can appreciate Christmas festivities.) I made a comment about how nice the bar looked with all the lights. He gave me a very skeptical look and said, "Wait… you're Jewish, right?" "Yes," I replied. "So you've never celebrated Christmas?" he said, somewhat aghast. "Nope, never," I said. "You didn't even have a *tree*?!" he said. I told him I never had. He shook his head and looked at me with deepest sympathy, touched my shoulder, and said, "Wow, that's so awful. It must be terrible to be a Jew." I guess he's not converting.

THE LANGUAGE OF LOVE

He complimented me on my vocabulary by saying, "My Korean ex-girlfriend wouldn't know that word."

ALL-AROUND HATER

I met a guy on the train and we exchanged numbers. Turns out he was the son of an African despot. We went out, and he spent our entire date saying how his race should be the dominant one and that someday "whitey will get it." He was also really rude to our waitress, who was wearing a semi-revealing top. That's when he told me that he "pities" women because "they need to be controlled." I stood up and walked out.

AT LEAST THEY WEREN'T GOING FOR TACOS

We were supposed to meet for dinner, and he texted me that he was running late because he got stuck at work. I told him that's fine and that I would get us a table. Twenty minutes later, he comes in and, before he even sits down, apologizes over and over for being late. I tell him it's fine and that I hadn't waited very long. Trying to be sympathetic, I ask him what happened at work. "Well," he says, "we were about to close when these Mexicans came in, and you know how slow Mexicans are…"

CHASING AMY

He spent most of dinner talking about how in love he was with his roommate, a teenage lesbian. He even showed me a handmade book he'd written and illustrated for her as a gift! When he complained about how things just weren't working out between them, which was why he was trying dating, I suggested it might have something to do with her, you know, being a lesbian. He responded with a rant about how "perverted" oral sex was generally, but especially between women.

A (NON-INGLORIOUS) BASTARD

I'm Jewish, and he was from Germany (a fact my grandmother might hold against him, but I didn't). That is, until he started ranting that "the Jews are responsible for all wars, the bad economy, everything bad."

TAKE BACK THE (DATE) NIGHT

My date told me he believed bad things only happen to people who sabotage themselves and secretly want bad things to happen to them. While I tried to spin it that having a positive outlook is generally good, I still told him that sometimes bad things just happen unavoidably. He then chose to illustrate his point by bringing up rape, saying that women who are raped set themselves up for it, and if we all just stopped thinking of rape as a bad thing, the world would be a happier, more relaxed place.

Awful First Dates: Hollywood Dispatch

"In my twenties, I went to meet my date at a really chic, fashionable restaurant. I wasn't dressed up necessarily, but I had on a nice shirt and jeans. My date showed up in cutoffs and a tank top. I knew half the people in the restaurant, who were all looking at me like '*Who* is this guy with Michael Kors?' It was so embarrassing. My tip: always have your first date at a casual place."

—Michael Kors

Chapter 6

MR. FAST FORWARD

A major cliché about women is that we're always complaining that men can't commit. Well, that's certainly an issue with some men—but the other end of the spectrum is just as off-putting. You want a man who is open to a loving relationship and not running away, screaming, at the prospect. But it's a rare woman who's not freaked out by a man who acts like making you his girlfriend is his last chance at happiness before he dies alone (though there's nothing in our lexicon that's the male equivalent of "spinster," these guys definitely act like you're their only option, and desperation is never sexy).

It's these nice guys—every woman seems to have one as a down-on-his-dating-luck friend—who come on way too strong. On the receiving end, it feels like it can go from flattering to stalking in twenty minutes flat. You start to wonder, "How is he really that sure I'm the love of his life when he's only known me for an appetizers course?" Or worse, "Maybe he's more into having a girlfriend than anything in particular about me." Or something which will surely make you bolt: "Maybe he thinks I'm way too good for him. Huh…maybe I am—I don't want to settle, so I gotta go get me someone better!" Either way, the night doesn't end in passionate embraces if he's ready to propose on the starting line.

Telling you he loves you or introducing you to his family would be so cute if he did it after you were together for six months. After six minutes, not so much. Generally, these guys are harmless, hapless, and well-meaning—but we still understand why you're too freaked out to date them.

SPEED RACER

At dinner, he blurts out, "Are you seeing anyone else?" I wasn't sure how to respond, so I tried to play it off by smiling and flirtatiously saying, "I'm seeing everyone." He goes, "It's just that I really enjoy our time together, and I'd like to know that I'm the only one you're spending time with." We'd known each other for an hour.

THE LOVER

We had a great blind date and afterward were making out. All of a sudden, he whispers in my ear, "I love you." I was a little drunk, so I thought I'd misheard him. But a few minutes later, he whispered it again. I got really uncomfortable and asked how he could love me if he didn't know my last name. He freaked out and, hitting himself in the forehead, mumbled, "STUPID! STUPID!" I got the feeling it wasn't the first time he'd done this.

ILL COMMUNICATION

We had a good (not great, but fine) time over dinner—he was awkward, but I mostly found it endearing. The next day, I got a text from him that said, "Are we exclusive?" I ignored it, not sure if it was a joke or he was nuts. He texted again: "I need to know—have another date tonight and not sure if I should cancel."

HIS WAY OR THE HIGHWAY

I met him at an IT conference and he asked for my email address. We wrote each other several times, but if I didn't respond to him right away, he would send me snippy follow-ups to make sure I'd gotten his email. Still, I gave him the benefit of the doubt and made plans to get dinner together. He suggested his favorite restaurant, which was near his house but nearly an hour away from mine. I said okay as long as he agreed to drive me home afterward so I wouldn't have to take the train by myself at night. After an okay dinner, we got in the car and he started with a barrage of questions about what I'm looking for in a man, how well I thought the date went, my dating history, you name it. I tried to laugh it off and change the subject, but he got really offended and said he didn't feel like driving me home anymore, dropped me off at the train station, and sped away.

MR. AND MRS. SMITH

We started emailing on an online dating site and he seemed nice enough. A few emails in, I asked his last name. He wrote back calling me Mrs. His Last Name (let's say Smith). I thought it was kind of like high school, where you'd draw that on your notebook, so I laughed it off. But then he wouldn't stop. In every communication after that, he referred to me as Mrs. Smith. I still decided to meet up with him, and when he saw me at the bar, he goes, "Over here, Mrs. Smith!" That's when I got the feeling he wasn't joking.

9-1-1, WHAT'S YOUR EMERGENCY?

After an amazing, ten-hour marathon first date, he dropped me off at my apartment and asked that I text him when I got inside that I was safe (we were parked literally beneath my window). I dutifully texted him and tossed the phone back into my purse. Some forty-five minutes later I thought it was weird he hadn't written me back. I looked at my phone and realized it hadn't gone through, so I resent it. A second later, he calls in a hysterical rage, screaming that he was terrified that something had happened to me. I assured him I was safe, and he shouted, "I even called 9-1-1, I was so worried!" Three days went by, then he texted me to ask, "Are we over? And, if so, is it because I called 9-1-1?"

THE APPLE DOESN'T FALL FAR...

By the time we ordered appetizers, he'd already told me, apropos of nothing, that everyone in his family was either an addict or mentally ill. His parents were raving alcoholics, and as a result of his childhood, he was on a strict regimen of medication for post-traumatic stress disorder. "No kid should be beaten with a garden hose," he said, digging into his salmon entrée. I agreed, of course, and felt bad for him, but it was getting a little deep for only knowing each other for twenty minutes. I suggested we change the subject to something lighter, but he put his hand on mine, gazed into my eyes, and said, "I want you to see what I've been through and love me for it." Check, please!

NOT TONIGHT, DUDE!

I gave a guy at the bar my number, and he texted me to make plans for the weekend. A few hours before we were supposed to meet, I wrote him and explained I (honestly) wasn't feeling well and that I'd need to reschedule. He completely panicked, sending me a series of texts: "Then maybe take a nap and see how you feel later? I don't know, kinda bummed right now to be honest…for me to cancel on someone I want to see in just a few hours, I would have to be in pretty rough shape." Trying to guilt me into going out wasn't working—I didn't respond—so he tried another tactic. "Or maybe you're not that excited about seeing the other person. I hope it is the prior one. The proverbial ball is in your court. I get that you're busy, but I'm a firm believer in that we make time for the things that we really want. I just thought that you would be excited about tonight. You can understand where I'm coming from, right?" Imagine that message loaded with winking emoticons.

AN INDECENT PROPOSAL

An old flame called me one night asking how I've been and would I like to go out this weekend? I hadn't seen him in a few months since we'd briefly dated, and I'd still been hung up on him after he stopped calling me. He was hot, smart, and shared my interests, as he'd come from Thailand to study in my same graduate program. At a fancy restaurant he picked, we caught up on each other's lives. He paid more attention to what I had to say that night than ever before, and I, flattered, kept talking. We were finishing up dinner, and he said, "Would you marry me for $10,000?" I told him that if we dated again I would consider marrying him, but why would he have to pay me? That's when he divulged his plan to fake a marriage so he could get citizenship and work in the U.S. after we graduated and his student visa expired. He said that taking a risk like this together would bond us and maybe turn into something meaningful. For him, the risk was basically nothing; if we were caught, then he would be deported back to Thailand, but I would face hefty fines and even prison. Of course I said no, and he spent the rest of the evening, until I finally got him to drop me off, trying to convince me to green-card-marry him.

HAWAIIAN TROPIC

He spends the entire dinner telling me exactly how much money he makes, obsessing about our age difference (twelve years), and then tops it off by saying that he closed his account to our mutual online dating service "as a compliment" to me (a little premature, buddy—it's our first date!). Then he invites me to spend the week with him in Hawaii when he goes for a conference in two days and tells me about a $1,500 bottle of cognac at his house that "we will drink and then you can go home." I finally manage to extricate myself without going home with him, but there is an email in my inbox when I arrive reiterating the Hawaii invitation.

HOUSEWIFE HUNTER

He told me that he was a financial analyst and his exact six-figure salary, which meant he made enough money that his wife would be able to stay home with his future kids, and asked if I'd be okay with agreeing to that. Fifteen minutes into our first date I'm not!

MAMA DRAMA

We met for coffee and, halfway through, his mother, who also lives in town, happened to show up. Instead of telling her he was on a date or that they'd talk later, he waved her over, and she slid into the booth next to me, ordered a coffee drink with alcohol in it, and spent the rest of our date getting tipsy and talking about which football teams she likes. She smoked a cigarette and accidentally ashed it into my cappuccino. Finally I decided to leave the two of them alone, so I said good night, and he walked me out the front door. When he tried to go in for a kiss, his mom started rapping on the window and cheering.

MAZEL TOV!

I was making plans for a first date with a guy I met on J-Date, the Jewish online dating site. I suggested something casual like drinks, or maybe coffee. Instead, he asked if I wanted to come to Rosh Hashanah dinner at his grandparents' house, two hours away.

THE OFFICE STALKER

There was a guy in my office who worked on another team but always hung around my department chatting and sometimes said hi to me. One day, he stopped by my desk and asked me to dinner. I had no idea what his name was, and I didn't find him particularly attractive, but he seemed nice, so I said okay.

He picks me up and takes me to the priciest restaurant

in the city, and after a few minutes, I can already tell there's no chemistry for me. Over appetizers, he says, "I've been watching you since the first day you started, on December 6," which was nearly two years before. Weird. Then he recounts exactly what I was wearing that day. He says he's asked everyone at work about me and that he "sees a real future for us." To let him down easy, I tell him I just got out of a bad relationship and don't want to be with anyone, but he persists, saying, "You're not going to change my mind. I'm determined to date you." I'm scrambling for what to say, so I suddenly blurt out a lie: "I can't date you...because I have herpes!" I'm mortified but I figure it will finally shake him loose. He pauses for a moment. Then he beams and says, "It's okay. I have herpes too!"

CHILD'S PLAY

He picked me up for our lunch date and drove us to a house. It turned out that the home belonged to his family, and that day his little brother was having his tenth birthday party. What we did on our "lunch date": watched *Teenage Mutant Ninja Turtles* with a bunch of ten-year-olds, watched them jump on the trampoline, and then we sat around the table with them while his mother served us pizza.

THAT ISN'T KOSHER

He told me that he couldn't have dinner with me because there were no kosher restaurants in my neighborhood. I'm Jewish too, but the I-eat-bacon-and-haven't-been-to-synagogue-since-my-Bat-Mitzvah kind. We agreed on dessert in his neighborhood instead, and over a piece of Rabbi-approved chocolate cake, I asked about his favorite books, movies, sports, music. He didn't like any of them. For fun, he said, he went to synagogue. I told him that we probably wouldn't make a great match, but he gazed into my eyes and told me that people can change. He walked me home in dead silence and, at my front stoop, took my hand. "I'm ready for a family," he said. "Are you?"

Awful First Dates: Hollywood Dispatch

"I fell asleep on his shoulder, and I slobbered and snored. That was pretty bad. But he shouldn't have taken me to see *There's Something About Mary* for my third time. Whoopsie."

—Kelly Rowland

Chapter 7
MR. TMI

Aren't women always saying we want a man who is open and honest, willing to share his utmost secrets, desires, dreams, and feelings? Well, yes. But that doesn't mean he needs to share them all at once, and certainly not within an hour of meeting you. These guys are chronic oversharers, spilling way more than we need to know, perhaps ever. No one wants a man who plays games, but there's something to be said for a little intrigue, a few mysteries that make you want to learn more about him. Maybe because they want to seem vulnerable, or for you to know their "true self," or just because they have a case of verbal diarrhea, these guys tell you more than you could ever want to know.

It's easy to identify Mr. TMI (too much information). Is

he sharing something that should only be admitted in front of a priest? Are you embarrassed for him? Are you spending the evening nodding and saying "mmm-hmmm" a lot, wondering if this is exactly what it feels like to be a shrink? Are you coming away from the evening knowing how he lost his virginity, what his ATM PIN is, his illegal activities, and having seen hundreds of photos of his childhood pet gerbil, Señor Stinky? Then your date needs to learn how to shut it.

WHAT A WEENIE

On the date, we proceeded to get very drunk. Then he started crying and confided to me about how small his penis was and asked if he could show it to me to get my opinion.

SCOOBY DON'T

Over dinner, he told me he'd put my photo on his website (he found it online) and that he'd already told his mom all about me and really, all he wanted to do was get married. He also informed me that I would be required to have as many children as possible, and he already had the names. He got progressively drunker and accused me of flirting with the waiting staff. The next day, he sent me a text with a picture of him dressed up as Scooby Doo for no reason. He called three weeks later, accusing me of giving him chlamydia. I had to explain it wasn't transmitted through kissing.

HE'S PORNY

We met at the library of all places and had a really intellectual talk about our favorite books. We exchanged numbers, and I called him a few days later to see if he wanted to meet up again. When I asked what he was doing, he said, "Not much—just watching some porn." I thought it was a joke until he asked if I wanted to come over and watch with him.

TUMMY TROUBLES

After dinner, he excuses himself to go to the bathroom, and I wait…and wait…and wait. He finally comes back, and I ask if he's okay; he says he's fine. We head back to my apartment to hang out, and he goes to the bathroom again. I wait and wait and wait again. He finally comes out, and I ask him if he's all right. He says he is. After he left, I discovered the wads and wads of toilet paper shoved in the corner—I guess because he was too embarrassed to flush the toilet over and over? Of course I never called him again.

HIGH TIMES

When I picked him up, he'd just gotten a hamburger and chips and proceeded to eat them in my car. (I thought we were going for a meal, so I hadn't eaten.) Then he asked if we could make a quick stop, so I followed his directions, and we ended up at his pot dealer's house. I sat there for an hour watching them smoke before I stood up and announced that I was leaving. He asked for a ride home and I said okay. Before he got out of the car, he asked, "Can I touch you 'down there'?" Needless to say, the answer was no.

BABY MAKER

He's twenty minutes late to dinner, and when he arrives, he insists on dining at one of the outdoor tables, even though I point out that it's sixty degrees and I'm wearing spaghetti straps. Within moments of sitting down, he asks why I don't have kids. He then tells me his sperm count and adds, "If you want to be a mother, I can help with that." I bail early but by the time I get home, I already have an email from him, complete with an attachment containing the results of his latest physical.

A BAD PREVIEW

Before our movie started, he told me he'd had only one relationship and she dumped him, leaving him so heart-broken he tried to kill himself. Halfway through the movie, he kept putting his hand on my leg, and I'd move it and he'd put it back. Then I was waiting for the bus home, and he decided to wait with me so he could show me every single photo in his phone of him and his ex together, describing where they were taken and how long they'd been together at that point.

FLOW-JOE

I was five minutes into a date with a new guy and we were covering the normal small talk: jobs, our neighborhoods, our apartments. After explaining that I lived with several female roommates, he asked if we were all on the same menstrual cycle.

HIGH EXPECTATIONS

We met for lunch and he kept going on about how fed up he was with living with his parents (he's forty and unemployed). He then informed me that I shouldn't be worried about his prospects—he would be ready to move out in a few months. And how was he planning to pay for this supposed big move with no job? With the profit he planned to make from the marijuana crop he's growing! He said he expected to make about ten grand, and that he does this every year, and it's no big deal. I told him that was weird and illegal, and that I wanted no part of it. After which he became sulky and wouldn't finish his lunch.

GET A HANKIE

While walking through the park, he kept sneezing and told me he had really bad allergies. I offered him a tissue from the packet in my purse. He turned it down—and then covered one of his nostrils to blow a snot rocket and said, "All better." No, sir, it is not.

HE NEEDS AN ALARM CLOCK, NOT A GIRLFRIEND

The guy I'd been talking to online emailed me on Friday to set up our date for the next morning—he suggested meeting at 11 a.m. at a neighborhood coffee shop. I was about to leave to meet him when I turned on my phone—he'd texted me at 3 a.m. saying he stayed out late drinking and would need me to call him in the morning (he'd set his ringer on loud) to wake him up or else he would "sleep all afternoon." I actually called him (it was ten minutes before we were supposed to meet) and he answered all groggy and said he was awake but was lying in bed watching TV.

I decided to cancel—our first conversation was me waking him up like I was his mom!

A RASH DECISION

We met for dinner and drinks, and I mentioned that I liked his beard; he told me he had a terrible neck rash and couldn't shave. We had a few glasses of wine, and as he got drunker, it came out that he was not only unemployed but was also homeless, couch-surfing, and still messing around with an ex-girlfriend whom he bitterly rambled on about for way too long. At the end of the night, he asked me to go "home" with him! Not excited at the prospect of waking up wedged into a couch next to a guy with a skin rash, I politely declined. Then he offered to come stay over at my house—and infect my pillows? No thank you.

DISHONORABLE DATE

As he drove me home, he told me how he had recently gotten out of the army. He (an enlisted soldier) was friends with a female officer, but another officer was jealous and so "made up a story" about how my date and this female officer were sleeping together (which can get you a dishonorable discharge pretty fast), so instead of going through that, he "pretended to be depressed" so he could get out for medical reasons instead of bad behavior.

PROZAC NATION

We agreed on meeting up after work for dinner and drinks. As I eyed the menu, I noticed that he hadn't touched his menu and asked, "What are you ordering for dinner?" He said, "Nothing. I've already eaten." Okayyy. Then I asked, "What are you drinking?" "Oh, I don't drink," he said. We'd been at the table fewer than five minutes. "I'm on Prozac because I'm absolutely crazy, and Prozac doesn't mix with alcohol."

SON OF DEBBIE DOWNER

I met this cute guy for a blind date at a coffee shop. From the beginning, his expression was mopey, and as soon as I sat down, he began methodically listing off every terrible thing that had happened to him in his life. His car got broken into, his band's equipment got stolen another time, his cat got run over by his mom when she came home drunk one night. I tried to look sympathetic, but I realized the only thing I was contributing to our conversation was, "Oh no, how terrible!" My breaking point with his sob stories was when he started describing how he once got kicked in the junk with another kid's cleat so now only has one testicle. I thanked him for the fun time and left.

THAT'S SOME HEAVY BAGGAGE

On our first date, he talked a lot about his ex-wife (except he'd sometimes refer to her as his wife), about how she left him, and his subsequent suicide attempts. When he said that, I touched his arm and said I was sorry. All of a sudden, he froze. He closed his eyes and started taking these big deep breaths. I asked if he was okay, and he said that he was so emotional because it had been five years since another human being had touched him.

THIS DATE BLOWS

I met a guy at a very noisy bar, so I had no idea that he talked that loudly in everyday life. On our date, sitting at a coffee shop, he yelled through the entire conversation, which was embarrassing enough…until he decided to tell a story about how when he was fourteen, he was flexible enough to give himself oral pleasure. I turned bright red and tried to change the subject, but he went on about how he used to do this all the time until he was no longer flexible enough to reach. The people around us looked like they were trying not to laugh…or vomit.

THE BOOKWORM

I'm an avid reader so I decided to ask him about his favorite novel. His response was, "I haven't read anything in a while. Well, maybe in high school?…Nope. Hmmm, maybe in middle school?…Nope. I may have read something in elementary school. Come to think of it, I have never read an entire book in my life."

FAMILY TIES

Things were going well—conversation was easy and we had a lot in common. I didn't realize how much, though, until he told me his rather unusual last name, and I asked him if he knew a woman in the city who had the same last name—who turned out to be his sister. And my gynecologist. Who recently treated me for herpes.

TOO-HONEST ABE

After a dinner heavy on pork belly, we went to a tequila bar, and two drinks in, my stomach started doing flips. I politely told my date that I wasn't feeling well (not mentioning specifics) and needed to head home. Ever the empathetic guy, he told me not to worry—he'd had diarrhea while on dates before.

HE'S A SAMANTHA

MY DATE: So I have to ask you something. It's extremely important.

ME: Okay…

MY DATE: When you go to Bloomingdale's, where is the first place you head?

ME: The second floor, I guess. Women's clothing.

MY DATE: Me too! I love women's fashion. I used to watch *Sex and the City* just to see all the clothes and shoes, like Manolo Blahniks. Do you have any Manolos?

THE PUPPET MASTER

He said he'd cook me dinner at his place. The apartment was sparse and not really decorated, like a typical guy's apartment, but the dining room walls were covered in ceramic Mardi Gras masks, and a marionette of a clown. I didn't even know what to say, so I asked why he had a marionette. "It was really expensive, but worth it," he said, "because I like to put on puppet shows."

THE AMATEUR DERMATOLOGIST

He told me he didn't really like his job, so I asked what his dream job would be. "I'd like to take care of people, to make them feel better," he said. I thought that might mean becoming a personal trainer or a nurse. "Maybe," he said, "but I really just like to help people feel good by taking care of their skin. Suppose you had a pimple on your face. I would like to pop it for you."

Awful First Dates: Hollywood Dispatch

"It's very odd to start dating after being married for a long time, and this was one of my first dates since the divorce from my husband. My date might have only been six or seven years older than me, but my kids see me as very youthful. He came to the door to take me out. My daughter was teeny tiny at the time, and she announced, 'Mom, he is too old for you' right in front of him."

—Andie MacDowell

Chapter 8

MR. MALADJUSTED

This is the type of man who makes you think you've gone crazy, even though he's the one acting a fool. He runs over animals and keeps driving; he says things that are completely inappropriate; in the middle of a fancy restaurant, he starts eating soup with his hands. I mean, who *does* that? These guys. Faced with this kind of date, you might worry you've hallucinated his behavior, that no one could seriously be *that* clueless. Or wonder if Ashton Kutcher is punk'ing you. Or figure that at least this will make a good story, if anyone will believe it. Or you start making excuses for your date: maybe he came from an "anytime is naked time" home, or he has undiagnosed Asperger's, or he's just a free spirit who doesn't feel constrained by societal norms, and good for him. Still, his wack-a-doodle behavior is too much to handle.

Dating should be about enjoying your time with a person you respect and are attracted to—not about rehabilitating a man who acts like he was raised by wolves and is only now entering civilization. You're looking for a partner, not *Encino Man*. So if he's lacking the kind of basic skills the rest of us mastered in elementary school, make a dash for the door. The good news is that he's probably too clueless about social cues to even know he's being ditched.

BLOODY PERFECT

He was fifteen minutes late, even though he'd told me on the phone he only lived two blocks from the restaurant. When he finally showed up, we shook hands and he said, "I'm sorry about my face." Noting nothing of offense, I asked why. He pointed out a teeny-tiny scar above his lip. He told me he'd gotten so drunk a month before that he woke up in his apartment covered in dried blood with a paper towel stuck to his face and never found out what happened. "The worst part is, that's not even the first time I woke up bloody this year," he continued. "In February, I woke up with a bloody hand at 6:30 a.m. on a subway platform." We hadn't even sat down yet.

DISAPPEARING ACT

We were half an hour into a great date. But in the middle of me talking, without him giving any reason (or even looking at his watch), he suddenly jumps off the bar stool and goes, "Okay, nice meeting you," throws down some cash, and runs off, leaving me sitting there with a nearly full beer. I stayed there to drink it, figuring you just can't hit it off with everyone. But the weirdest part was that when I got home I already had an email from him saying what a nice time he'd had and asking me out again.

FRO-YO IS A NO-GO

I was happy to meet my set-up: tall, handsome, and passionate about desserts. He was opening his own frozen yogurt store in a few weeks and suggested we get fro-yo at a busy competitor's place. Once we got inside, he completely ignored me, hounding the other customers in line about why they chose this place, their flavor prefer-ences, and even handed strangers his business cards, saying they should come to him instead. The only time he talked to me was to analyze my thoughts on their topping offerings.

THE DAREDEVIL

He seemed like a pretty responsible, down-to-earth guy: he liked sports, worked in finance, and took me to dinner at TGIFridays. But on the way home, he started showing off by driving down one of the busiest roads in town with no hands on the steering wheel. He really thought he was impressing me, and as we swerved over the center line, he asked, "So, do you like bad boys?"

CALL HIM KERMIT

When I showed up for our date, he was reading a book of poetry—and started reading to me aloud. After our drinks, we decided to walk down to a sidewalk sale to do some people watching. There he bought a frog hand-puppet. For the rest of the date, every time he talked, it would be through the puppet. We stopped at a coffee shop and I ordered a drink. Then he held up his puppeted hand and, in a squeaky frog voice, told the barista, "I'd like one too, please!"

MAGIC MAN

I was set up with a guy my friend told me was a lawyer, since I'm one also...but it turns out when I asked him about it, he defines himself more by his hobby: being a magician. I thought it was kind of odd and didn't know what to say, so I jokingly asked if he was going to cast a spell on me, making me fall in love with him. He got really offended and started lecturing me, his voice rising to the point that other people in the bar were turning around and looking at us, that only *witches* cast spells.

NOT-SO-SILENT BOB

A friend asked if I'd like to be part of a silent date auction, just using my photo and bio, to benefit his nonprofit, and I agreed. A few days later, he sent me an email connecting me with the winner, DJ Valentine (who, as it turns out, had actually never DJ'd). When we met up, I could see why the guy had participated in a silent auction: he talked nonstop, without even pausing to breathe in between thoughts. I asked him about work; he said, "I hate my job because I hate helping people. I want to work with less human inter-action." So I asked him about his hobbies outside of work, and he told me, "I do jujitsu in the mornings. Monday and Tuesday morning. Wednesday after work. Thursday and Friday mornings. What I've learned is that you have to cut your nails really short or else they'll rip off." His other major hobby? "Sleeping on the subway. Sometimes I wake up at 7 a.m. and I've just been going back and forth on the train all night." I tried to excuse myself four times, but he wouldn't stop rambling enough for me to even finish saying I needed to head out. Eventually I got so fed up I grabbed my coat and said, "It's late—gotta run!" and bolted out of there.

MAYBE HE'S IN THE FBI?

At brunch, the waiter passed me a note with the bill, asking me out. I thought it was kind of ballsy and cute, so I called him and we set up a date to meet for coffee. But once we got there, the guy refused to tell me anything about himself and kept dodging anything I asked. I'd say, "So, how long have you lived here?" and he would say, "Oh, on and off for years." When I asked, "Where are you from?" he said vaguely, "My family has lived all over." He didn't want to tell me his last name, how old he was, or anything else you find out when you're getting to know someone. When I said it was kind of strange that he was hesitant to talk yet he'd asked me out, he told me he'd prefer to "keep the conversation more general, philosophical." Oh, really? Because I'd prefer to end it.

HE'S PUZZLING

After a pleasant dinner, the guy seemed a little nerdy and awkward, but I waved it off as endearing. We went back to his apartment and he showed me around. His bedroom was lined with action figures and comic-book posters, which seemed a little immature and more nerdy than I'd expected, but okay. I was hoping we might make out for a little in his bedroom, but he was eager to take me somewhere else: the empty dining room. That is, the room that was empty except for a gigantic framed jigsaw puzzle on the wall, depicting the Simpsons sitting for *The Last Supper*. Maybe I could also get over that the guy spent a lot of his free time putting together puzzles. But the red velvet rope in front of it, so I didn't get too close like it was a priceless Picasso, put me over the edge.

HE'S STRIKING OUT

During dinner he informed me he had been to the dentist that day and was all loopy from the pain meds he'd gotten—which would explain why he kept dribbling his soup. Afterward, we went bowling and he kept trying to stand behind me and "guide" my arm to show me how to get a strike, yet didn't seem to notice that my score was actually better than his. In between frames, he proceeded to tell me about how he makes money despite being unemployed: he scams buyers on eBay by making another account and fake bidding to drive up the price. He was very proud of himself for coming up with that one and kept rambling and doing loopy laughs, which I hope was from the pain medicine.

BAG IT!

I went out with a guy who was really hot and tough—he built motorcycles. On the date, he asked me a lot of questions about what countries I'd been to, and I thought it was cool he was so interested in travel. We went back to his apartment and he pulled out a big plastic box the size of a moving trunk. I had no idea what he was going to show me, and it turned out to be his most prized possession: his chip bag collection. The guy was obsessed with collecting potato chip bags from all around the world. He told me that he had the second most in the world, according to Guinness World Records. Trying to feign interest, I asked if I could see some of his favorite ones, but he said they would all inflate if you took the lid off.

AWFUL FIRST NOT-DATE

A guy I knew liked me—he followed me around school, always complimented me and tried to touch my arm when we talked, and repeatedly asked me to prom. I said no because I didn't have feelings for him and my parents wouldn't let me date yet, so I was just going with friends. On the day of prom, my friends and I congregated at one of our houses, and he was part of the group. Even though I'd told him I wasn't going with him, he'd brought me a corsage, introduced me to his mother as his girlfriend, and hung around me the entire night. When I stood up to dance with the rest of my single friends, he would always come and dance next to me; everyone thought I was his date. When people asked him if we came to prom together, he'd tell them yes, because technically we'd ridden there in the same limo.

A REAL T-BONER

My parents pressured me into a date with a friend of a friend's son, who went by the nickname T-Bone. I assured my parents that though I was living in the south, it didn't mean I would date someone named T-Bone, but they told me I was being a snob and so, to prove them wrong, I went. He suggested meeting at a chain steakhouse called T-Bones; I could not make this up. When we met for dinner, I was surprised to find that he was missing two front teeth. He told me about the double-wide trailer he lived in on his father's property and proudly told me about his pet goat. I'm an animal lover, so this was kind of redeeming, until he told me that he kind of hated the goat but kept it around so he wouldn't have to mow the lawn. We made small talk about my job as a Latin teacher. He responded by telling me he was fascinated because he's always wanted to visit Latin America. Sigh.

SHOW-STOPPING PERFORMANCE

He seemed great and asked me out to dinner and an improv comedy show. An hour before he was supposed to pick me up, he texted that he wasn't hungry and we should just meet at the show. I sort of frowned at that, but I refused to let the little setback dampen my mood. When he picked me up and we headed over to the theater, he was a lot quieter than usual. He sat stiffly in his seat, didn't move, and eventually started clutching his stomach. I pretended not to notice, but what I couldn't ignore was the vomit that started spurting everywhere—he leaped out of his chair, clapped a hand over his mouth, and bolted for the door in the middle of the show. I felt awful about it and followed him outside. When he stopped barfing, I asked if he was okay. He said, "That's why I didn't want to go to dinner," and went to wash up in the bathroom. When he came out, I said we should go and get together another time, but he insisted on returning to our seats and watching the rest of the show.

THE NEXT SCORSESE

He chatted me up online, saying he was a film director. The night before the date, he sent me a link to some of the "short films" he directed, which were basically him using a camera on a tripod to creepily film himself in an empty room. One featured him singing a song about how girls aren't nice to him, in which he appeared as both the man and, in full drag, as the woman.

THE TIME BANDIT

We had dinner, watched TV, and drank too much red wine. We ended up messing around on the couch and I took off my designer watch, which I loved and my mom had given me, and put it on the coffee table. I took a taxi home and called him the next morning to ask about when I could see him next to get my watch. He claimed it wasn't on the table and he'd never seen it, and didn't return my calls after that. WTF, watch-stealer!

SKIN DEEP

When we made plans to meet up in person after talking on an online dating site, he mentioned he had a "mild skin condition," which I figured was light acne or a birthmark or something. When he showed up, he had flakes of skin flapping in the wind, bleeding cracks around his mouth… anything but "mild."

BUNNY KILLER=PSYCHO KILLER

As he was driving us to the restaurant, he swerved to hit a bunny rabbit. I started yelling that you're supposed to swerve to *avoid* hitting animals. That's when he explained to me that he thinks it's funny because every time he and his friends do it, they earn "points" with each other, and he needed two more points "to take the lead."

IT SLEEPS TWO

After dinner, we went to his place so he could drop something off, and while he was in the kitchen, I decided to peek
in and check out his bedroom. When I flipped on the light,
a man started yelling—it was his dad, who was asleep in his
bed. My date ran in to explain who I was. I asked why his
dad was in his room (it was a one-bedroom apartment, and
my date was thirty), and he explained that they shared the
bed; his dad worked the graveyard shift so slept in it during
the day, and since my date worked days, he explained, "I
have the bed overnight, so we can still get freaky." On
sheets warm from his dad.

HE'LL HAUNT YOUR DREAMS

I met a cute guy at a friend's party. I went to his place and
we cooked dinner together. We talked for a few hours and
then suddenly I got very tired and started to feel really sick
(I have a chronic medical condition). So I explained why I
felt sick and asked if I could crash there, but made it clear
we would not be hooking up. He said of course, lent me

some pajamas, and I went to sleep. I woke up a little later to him dry-humping my leg and whispering scary stories about his ex and their violent breakup. I was in too much pain to drive myself home or really even think straight, so I just pushed him off me several times and left as soon as I felt up to it, around dawn. He continued to call and email me for months, sending things he'd found about me online, like papers I had written in college.

FEELIN' GROOVY

I made plans with a folk singer who worked at a local record store and seemed pleasantly laid-back. Well, laid-back was an understatement. When he picked me up for our date, he was clearly stoned, and he had to throw a bunch of junk off his (broken) passenger seat for me to sit down. Then he grabbed a two-gallon jug of warm juice out of the backseat and offered me a swig. I declined and asked what he had planned for our date. He said, "I think we should hang out in the woods and just groove on each other."

NOT A SEAT SAVER

We went to the movies, and there were still a few seats in one of the middle rows. For some reason, my date tried to drag me to the very front row, where you have to sit looking straight up at the screen the whole time. I refused and took a seat in the middle of the theater…but instead of sitting with me, he marched down to the front row and spent the whole movie sitting by himself, sulking and turning around to glare at me.

A TOTAL KNOCKOUT!

After our date, we met up with some of our mutual friends. He was goofing around, play-fighting with another guy. My date swung a punch, somehow missed our friend, and hit me square in the face. He kept apologizing, but when I woke up with a huge black eye the next morning, he asked me not to tell people it was from him.

LET'S CALL HIM CLIFF

I'm an English professor, so I said in my online dating profile that a shared love of books is important to me. Over dinner, I asked my date what his favorite book was. His reply: "*1984*." Which is fine, but kind of high-school-age reading. So I asked him why it still stood out for him, and he said, "Well, I haven't actually read it. I read the *CliffsNotes*. But I could tell that if I did read it, it would definitely be my favorite."

THE GROOMING GUY

I ran into a guy I knew from a few years back and he invited me to go to the beach with him. When I got to his house, he had me sit and watch a game on TV, that I had no interest in, for two hours. Then he invited his four roommates to come with us to go swimming—not so romantic. When we got back to their apartment, my date sat back down to watch even more sports and *clip his toenails* in front of me while watching the game. At one point, he even sneezed into his hand and looked at it before wiping it on his swim trunks. Disgusted, I left to go home, and right before I shut the door, he yelled, "Call me!"

JEALOUS OF WHAT?

We both liked to dance, so we agreed to go out for a light meal and then go a club. But when we met up, he said his back hurt so we had to skip dancing. So we went to dinner, where he proceeded to tell me how he had just lost his job—apparently his boss was a terrible bitch who fired him because she was jealous of him. Then he told me he was still in love with his ex-girlfriend, that she was his soul mate, but the problem was that she was a bad kisser. He then asked if I could demonstrate for her how it was done and pulled out his phone to try to record himself kissing me. When I pulled away, he started cursing at me and telling me I was an ugly bitch with (surprise!) a jealousy problem.

THE FAIRY KING

We met at the shoe store where he was a sales clerk. But during our first date, he informed me that actually his true calling was being a sculptor. I asked how he got into it, and he went into this monologue:

"When I was a kid, my class had to do reports, and one girl did hers about fairies. She said that at first she didn't believe the fairies were real, but then she saw some in her grandmother's backyard. But the teacher hated her report and said that fairies weren't real. Her face fell, and in that moment I decided that I would *make* her believe in fairies again. [At this point tears are welling up in his eyes.] So I went home that afternoon, went into my backyard, and found some dead birds. I mean, they were already dead—I didn't kill them myself or anything. And I took them inside and boiled off the skin, then used the bones to *build* her a fairy!"

I'm not sure what he said after this, because after the boiling-dead-birds thing, my mind was pretty occupied with planning my escape.

THIS DATE ROCKS

While we were talking, I noticed he was sort of chewing on something, but it didn't look like gum. I asked him what was in his mouth, and he pulled out a *rock*. He told me he chews on them to "keep him grounded"…because he finds them on the ground.

HE'S NOT PLAYING POSSUM

He asked me out to swing-dance, which I love. He picked me up in a church minivan and took me to the "dance hall," which turned out to be his church. He introduced me to everyone as his girlfriend. When he finally agreed to dance, he trampled all over my feet and complained that we would be great if I only "knew how to follow." I told him I wanted to leave. He was driving the minivan dangerously fast, talking about what a great driver he was, when he ran down a possum with a terrible crunch. I was devastated, but his reaction was deranged giggling. The high-pitched laughter continued all the way home, at which point he insisted on walking me to the door and actually dared trying to kiss me. Then he invited me to youth group that Sunday.

ANGER MANAGEMENT

When he arrived to pick me up, he announced that our first stop would have to be the mall, because he needed a belt. (I don't know why he didn't get the belt before picking me up, but I tried to be open-minded.) After the mall, we headed to the restaurant, and it started to rain. His windshield wipers didn't work, which made him start shouting and cursing. Upon arriving at the hibachi-style restaurant, he was irritated to find we'd be seated with strangers and refused their offer of an extra restaurant coupon, taking it as an insult that he couldn't afford dinner. Afterward, he stopped at a gas station to buy gum (probably thinking I'd make out with him), and was furious to find that it had already closed, so he started yelling and banging his fists on the door.

(GRAND)MAMA'S BOY

After dinner, we decide to go back to his place. He pulls up to a really big, fancy house, and leads me up to his room with a huge fancy waterbed; I think he's done really well for himself to have a place this nice. I figured, worst comes to worst, he still lives with his parents. We're making out when a lady starts yelling in the other room about the television. He says, "Oh no! I didn't know Grandma was home. This is her room!"

THE SOUND OF SILENCE

As I walked to meet my date at the bar, a bird crapped on me, covering my hair and outfit in bird poo (I should have taken that as an omen). Once we'd been sitting together for a while, I realized that I was doing all the chatting and breaking every awkward silence, so I decided to see how long we would go without speaking if I didn't fill the space. The answer? Twelve and a half minutes. Then I left.

TURNING JAPANESE

He'd studied abroad in Japan, which he decided to show off by speaking to me only in Japanese (I don't speak any). I took him to a party at my friend's house, which he thought was apparently the perfect venue to do tai chi and try to quietly meditate right in the middle of it.

LIGHT ME UP

This may have been the shortest date ever. I picked him up at his house and, as I pulled out of the driveway, he pulled out a cigarette. I'm not a smoker, so I said, "I prefer if you didn't smoke in my car." He took out his lighter and lit the cigarette anyway, so I pulled back in the driveway and asked him to get out.

A GROOVY DEAL-BREAKER

I met a seemingly nice, normal guy for drinks at a trendy new wine bar. We had good conversation, shared our food, opined about the wine, etc. I was excited that he called me the next day…until he told me that I was "a grave disappointment" and ultimately undateable because I had somehow conveyed to him the previous night that I wouldn't want to dress up in full 1970s costume and accompany him to a KC and the Sunshine Band concert.

GOOD-BYE, NEWMAN!

MY DATE: Wow, I'm firing questions at you like an interview. Seinfeld said the only difference between a date and an interview is that you have a chance of getting naked at the end of the date. [laughs hysterically]

MY DATE, AGAIN [noting that I'm not laughing]: Are you familiar with Jerry Seinfeld?

ME: Yes.

MY DATE: Well, he said the only difference between a date and an interview is that you have a chance of getting naked at the end of the date! [laughs hysterically again]

That was our best conversation.

THE ATTENTION JUNKIE

As we drove away from my building, he catcalled at the supermodel who lived downstairs from me; then he confessed the most interesting thing about him was that his sister was famous. He thought Benihana would be fun for dinner, and when we got there, he tried to force our table into a communal discussion about why I should like him. When he got up to use the bathroom, they all encouraged me to "just leave." When he dropped me off, he couldn't understand why I wasn't inviting him up. (I mean, hadn't he mentioned that his sister was famous?)

PAGING DR. FREUD!

All he could talk about was how hot his mom was. And how his friends all thought she was hot. And how he couldn't imagine meeting anyone as hot as his mom.

DOUBLE SURPRISE

He told me our first date would be a surprise—and I certainly was surprised when he picked me up with the car full of his friends. I reluctantly climbed in, hoping this wouldn't turn out like a Lifetime movie. They refused to tell me where we were headed. After stopping to pick up earplugs (?!), we drove for another hour and a half, my stomach turning, until we pulled up at…a monster truck rally. It wasn't really my scene, but I seriously was *such* a good sport that I figured we'd definitely be going out again. The guy called the next day to say he was getting back together with his ex.

Awful First Dates: Hollywood Dispatch

"I was having dinner with a girl in a restaurant, and I was so incredibly bored—I had to get out. So I told her I had a business meeting I'd forgotten about and had to leave right then. I certainly don't think she bought it—luckily I never talked to her again."

—Tommy Hilfiger

Chapter 9
MR. CRITICAL

There's a funny old joke: "Before you criticize someone, you should walk a mile in his shoes. That way, when you criticize him, you're a mile away, and you have his shoes." This guy, though, doesn't mind criticizing his date right to her face. Before he even really knows her. Maybe he's trying to assert his dominance by putting her in a lowly can't-do-anything-right position. Maybe he's just a very candid person, and he truly thinks he's helping you by sharing his honest opinion. Whether he's trying to be harmful or helpful, you don't have to sit there and take it. I mean, who died and made him Judge Judy?

A lot of women struggle with self-esteem—and it's no wonder, if the people who are supposed to like us end up insulting us. A surprising number of know-it-alls want to ask you out, only to inform you that everything you do, like, or think isn't good enough. Thanks, dude, but we already have bitchy girlfriends and our mothers for that.

NO FAT CHICKS

I called to tell him I had just parked at the restaurant; he said he had too. I said I'd meet him in front of the entrance. After about ten minutes, I started getting concerned. I called him, but it went right to voicemail. I texted him; no answer. A few minutes later, he finally got out of his car and we went inside. We had decent conversation, but I didn't feel any chemistry. When I got home, he texted to ask me out again. I wrote back that I was sorry, but I just didn't think we had enough in common. He responded by saying that he disagreed, but it didn't matter because I was too fat for him anyway...which was why it took him ten minutes to get from his car to the door of the restaurant. He said he saw me standing there and couldn't decide whether to dash or not.

VERY ENCOURAGING

My date started off well, since he looked like the rapper Common (on that basis alone I was willing to overlook the fact he showed up forty minutes late). After we ordered, I admitted I don't exercise often, but to make up for that, I'm careful with what I eat. He responded, "It's a good thing you don't mind being fat." The worst part was that he honestly thought he was being encouraging.

AT LEAST HE'S WALKING

When I arrived on time at the bar we agreed to meet at, the bartender informed me my date had already been there for three hours. To make conversation, I told my date that my hobby is running; he called me "a jackass." I mentioned my favorite band; he said, "You're an idiot" and gave me the finger. Okayyyy, great conversationalist. Not long into the date, he admitted that he was an alcoholic and repeatedly tried to grab me. I left to walk to my car and cringed as he walked into traffic, making cars swerve and honk at him as the rest of the bar watched in horror.

LAUGHABLY LAME

I went on a date with a guy I met online. We walked around the mall, where he proceeded to tell me how "lame" everything I liked was. Then we drove to dinner, and he made fun of how "lame" my car was. The date ended with us walking out of the parking lot and him saying, "That dinner was so good, *I just want to take a dump so I can eat it all over again*." Then he tried to kiss me—lame!

LORD OF THE DANCE

The guy invited me to an Armenian festival, which I assumed was for the food and cultural experience. He never mentioned that it was because he's obsessed with Armenian dancing. So when I showed up and he saw that I walk with a cane, he was obviously put out. I explained that I could dance a bit, just not super enthusiastically all night, but he seemed uninterested. Then he excused himself to the bathroom, from where he texted me that he "wasn't feeling well" and had decided to go home, leaving me an hour from my apartment, alone, at an Armenian festival.

IS HE BENJAMIN BUTTON?

He came from out of town to visit me for the weekend, and things were going well…until he started comparing me to his ex-girlfriend. I didn't measure up, it seemed, as he proceeded to unfavorably compare my shower, my mattress, and even my pubic hair to those of his ex. When I saw his profile on a dating site a few months later, he'd miraculously shaved fifteen years off his age.

A BLONDE WOULD HAVE MORE FUN

We had mutual friends, and he asked me out over IM (I later found out he heard I was easy and wanted to try). We went to dinner, and after sitting in silence through our appetizers, he asked me what my ideal guy is like. I went into a lengthy explanation about qualities, interests, values, etc. Then I asked him what his dream girl is like. He said, "Blonde." I'm a brunette.

CAN YOU HEAR ME NOW?

We met up to walk around a nearby park. We passed a cell phone on the ground, and he picked it up—I thought he was going to be a good Samaritan and try to return it. Instead, he put it in his pocket and said, "Awesome. Free phone." As we continued walking, he seemed distracted and like he was bored. At one point, I told him that I'm a bit of a Trekkie and he just flat-out said, "Yeah. I have absolutely no interest in what you're talking about."

MAGICAL MYSTERY TOUR

We decided to go out to a nice dinner for our first date, so I dressed up: a dress, high heels. He picked me up in his huge pickup truck, which I struggled to climb into without flashing the street, while he sat in the driver's seat complaining about how long it took me to get in. After dinner, he decided to take me on a driving tour of his hometown, spending an hour in traffic pointing out every single spot of "significance" in his life: his paper route as an eleven-year-old, his tenth grade history teacher's house, etc. We also drove by his mother's house…which was when he told me he actually lived in a camper in her backyard so that he could still have her cook his meals and do his laundry. I thanked him for dinner but said that I didn't think it was going to work out. He then sent me an angry email every day for two weeks listing all the reasons I was unacceptable to him!

MAYBE IT WAS THE WRONG CAR?

We met online and had emailed for a few weeks, with both of us posting pictures. On the day we decided to meet, it was pouring down rain. He called to say he was outside in the car, so I ran out to meet him. I got in, my hair dripping wet, and said hello. His response: "Sorry, I'm not interested." He unlocked the doors and barely waited for me to get out of the car before he took off.

WAS HE GOING TO GUESS?

He was an interesting enough guy, very well-read. I asked him what his favorite book of all time was, and he said *The Celestine Prophecy*, because it made him see life differently. I started to tell him about my favorite book, but before I barely got a syllable out of my mouth, he shushed me.

ANALYZE THIS

I was on a date with a guy who worked as a psychologist, and we had some interesting discussions about people and relationships. At the end of the date, we ran into my ex. The

shrink insisted that we all sit down so he could analyze our relationship and why we broke up, which he did for the next forty-five minutes.

NOT A MAMA'S BOY

I'd known him for a few weeks so was excited when he asked me out to a yoga class. But the whole time, he acted weird and awkward, so I asked, "Is something wrong?" He said, "I'm not interested in pursuing this relationship as long as you are living with your mother." He, on the other hand, was currently living in his '76 VW Microbus, which was parked at a local hostel.

FIRST DATE TOPICS TO AVOID: EUGENICS

The dinner date was going well until he began to tell me about his "checklist." He seemed very excited that I met many of his criteria, telling me quite earnestly that he wanted attractive, tall children and would do whatever it took to secure that. I'm 5'9", and he said my height was a plus and he liked that I was slim. I tried to joke that he was making me sound like a brood mare, and he reached across the table, took my hand, and asked if, as the potential mother of his children, I would ever consider plastic surgery.

THE MATCHMAKER

I went out on a blind date with a guy who was hot and fun. I really liked him, but it was clear that he wasn't as into it. Oh well, it happens sometimes. When he texted me, just five minutes after we parted ways, to say that he had a good time but wasn't feeling it romantically, I thought it was a bit unnecessary—his feelings, or lack thereof, were pretty obvious—but I couldn't begrudge the guy for being honest with me. The next day, he texted me again to tell me that he'd thought it over and realized I might hit it off with his younger brother—would I like his number instead? Insult, meet injury.

THE CAREER COUNSELOR

We bonded over our family lives and senses of humor. He was funny and relaxed—until I mentioned that I work in publishing. He picked up his drink, pushed back his chair, put up his feet, and proceeded to give me a grandfatherly lecture about how books and magazines were going out of business and I likely wouldn't have a job this time next year.

VERY COMPLIMENTARY

I was totally smitten when he started listing the things he liked about me—my smile, my glasses. Then he goes, "The only bad thing is that your fingers are fat."

SPORTY SPICE

I met a guy on my marathon-training team who asked me out to dinner for the next night. I ordered, starting with a Diet Coke. He sneered and looked at me in disbelief, finally sputtering: "But I thought you were a runner!" Um, it's not like I was filling my CamelBak with the stuff. I explained  as much, and he retorted that soda was "full of chemical crap" and he "prefers a woman who takes care of her body."

THE POET

He took me to a poetry reading—we were twenty minutes late, because he'd forgotten to print out directions, but that turned out to be fine because the reading went on for another two and a half hours (and there were only three other people in the audience). When it was finally over, I asked if he wanted to get a drink, but he said I didn't look "fully engaged" in the reading. If I wanted to hook up sometime, that was cool, but for a relationship he was really looking for someone who took literature more seriously.

THE ANGRY ATHEIST

Over coffee, he asked me about my religious views, so I explained I was raised Christian and believe in God, although I no longer go to church except on holidays. Before I could even finish, he started to rant about how any smart person would deduce that there is no God. When I tried to change the subject, he asked me what my thoughts were about abortion.

EVERYONE'S A CRITIC

He wasn't exactly perfect—he'd arranged our date via text message, suggested we go to Chili's, and showed up ten minutes late. But within the first five minutes of conversation, he felt superior enough to nitpick everything I said. He insulted my choice of wine ("You might as well order grape juice if you're going to order white."), my eating habits ("You don't eat meat but you do eat fish? That just doesn't make sense."). To top it all off, he even managed to criticize *the hospital where I volunteer* ("My friend had an *awful* experience there."). I wanted to tell him I was having an awful experience here.

THE SELF-ESTEEM BUILDER

We started to make out, but I didn't want to go further, so I got up to leave. He followed me to the door and said I was obviously just leaving because I was too insecure to get naked in front of him. I rolled my eyes, so he dissected my entire outfit: "You're wearing high heels, which means you're insecure about your height. And don't even get me started on your padded bra…"

THE TROUBLE WITH TWITTER

My date seemed to be sending a lot of text messages while we were at dinner. Annoyed, I asked if it was work-related and if he really needed his phone out the whole time. He said yes, because he was live-blogging our whole date on Twitter, down to what I was wearing and how long it took me to decide what to order.

HOOFING IT

He offered to come "pick me up for dinner." You can imagine my surprise when he showed up at my place on *foot* (apparently he didn't own a car, a detail he conveniently left out). I'm all for going green, but I was wearing heels, so I wasn't too jazzed about walking a bazillion blocks just to dine at some generic Italian restaurant where he'd made a reservation. Though I never complained, I eventually started to limp, at which point he started to rant about why girls always wear such uncomfortable shoes.

Awful First Dates: Hollywood Dispatch

"I went bowling on a double date...I got excited and I accidentally threw the ball the wrong way—backward. It was so embarrassing. They were like, 'Yeah, she's so uncool.'"

—singer Jessie J

Chapter 10

MR. OUT-TO-DINNER DISASTER

We've already covered how weird guys can get about who pays for dinner, but lots of them screw up the date far before the check comes out. Some of them think it's romantic to order for you—the thing is, when he's known you for ten minutes (not long enough to learn you're a vegetarian) and orders you the veal parmesan, or says you'll be having a martini when you're really more of a red-wine type, the practice just seems antiquated, even arrogant. Other guys ruin their second-date chances with their table manners. We're not asking for Emily Post-level etiquette; in fact, we'd settle for guys who don't make pasta into finger food or insist that belching is a compliment to the chef.

THE DINNER DECIDER

He was forty-five minutes late to the restaurant where we were supposed to meet for dinner. I wouldn't have waited, except that he called every five minutes saying he was only a minute or two away, so I should sit tight. He eventually arrived and while we were waiting for our food, I went to the bathroom. While I was gone, our food had come out… except he'd sent mine back because he decided "it didn't look good." While he sat there and ate, he kept putting big blobs of mashed potatoes on my plate, insisting, "I really want to watch you eat this." Then when the waitress came back and we ordered our second round of drinks, he told her to use less vodka in mine because he didn't want me to get too tipsy and "make a scene." After that, I politely excused myself. He left me so many messages in the next week that I ended up having to change my phone number!

BUT IS HE A DOUBLE DIPPER?

I met this guy for a drink and we decided to share an appetizer of hot spinach-artichoke dip. It came with a handful of pita-bread triangles, and he ate all but one of them, which he so graciously let me have. Since there was so much dip left, I was about to ask the server for more bread, when I saw him grab the bowl of dip and sink his fingers into it. He then ate the entire bowl of dip with his index and middle finger, wiping the bowl clean.

WINGING IT

I had been chatting with a guy online and our attempts to meet kept running into scheduling problems, so I was excited when he texted me one evening that he was at a local bar and I should come by, since I happened to be free. I walk in and spot the guy—he's wearing a fedora and he's up to his elbows in a huge platter of chicken wings. Without even looking up from eating, he offers me some wings. No thanks. I order a glass of water. I stand there for a few minutes while he's hoovering up the wings and ignoring me… then I say, "Um, you know, it's actually kind of late and I'm just gonna go on home." Again, he doesn't even look up but says, "Okay, see ya!" The next day he texted me to say, "I'm so glad we met…want to get together again?"

WE FEAR LEVEL 10

While driving me to dinner, he took three phone calls back to back and ignored me. He kept bragging about how lucky I was he decided to go out with me that night as everyone was dying to have him show up at their clubs and parties. We got to the quiet bistro, and he couldn't seem to get the waiter's attention, so he yelled "YO!" startling everyone, me included. He told the waiter we were ignored because we were black. He pulled the race card on a black waiter! Then he took three more calls over dinner. At the end of the night, I was dying to escape, and he told me again how lucky I was that he'd toned down his ego to a level 3, as he's usually a level 10.

BIKER BOY

On the night of our date, he showed up an hour late to pick me up. When he did show up, he just stayed outside my house on his motorcycle and beeped the horn. I ignored him until he came to the door. We took off on the motorcycle, I thought to dinner, but he ended up driving us around for an hour, at times in the rain. When we eventually stopped, he said, "I worked out today, so I need to eat some chicken. Is there a fried chicken place near your place?" I told him I was vegetarian. Still, he drove us to the fast-food place, bought a whole chicken (I didn't get anything), and then invited himself back to my house. He ate the chicken with his fingers and without a plate. After he finished eating, he walked over to my DVDs, pulled out a movie, and put it on without asking me. I told him I had to get up early, but he didn't seem concerned. After the movie, I thought he'd finally leave, but he put on the TV and watched until 1 a.m.! I tried several times to get rid of him, saying I was really tired and needed to go to bed. In the end, I had to actually walk over to the door, open it, and say, "Please leave."

SICK...OF YOU

I met a really cute guy at a bar, and we exchanged numbers. After texting for a few days, we made a Saturday night dinner date, and he said he'd pick me up. When I got into his car, I realized how thick my beer goggles must have been. Also, his heat was turned up crazy high. I soon understood why: he was extremely feverish and shivering to the point of his hands shaking. He told me he'd spent the entire day in bed and had taken four extra-strength painkillers (note: he was *driving* us to the restaurant) before picking me up so he wouldn't have to cancel the date. Kind of sweet, but he was really sick, and when I promised we could reschedule, he refused to take me home and headed on to the restaurant, driving like a crazy person. At dinner, not only did he order my meal without consulting me, but he also sat there shivering with his coat on, watching me eat, because by this time he was feeling too sick and weak to eat anything himself. When he dropped me off, he actually had the gall to ask for a good-night kiss. No, thanks—I don't need your swine flu!

YOU SAY POTAYTO,
I SAY POTAHTO

He said he knew a great place we could go for dinner that had amazing steaks and baked potatoes, so I accepted. He picked me up at my apartment and drove about twenty-five minutes. He asked me to close my eyes as we pulled in the parking lot because it was a surprise. When I opened my eyes, we were parked in front of a Wendy's. (I also want to point out there was a Wendy's five minutes from my house, so we drove all the way for nothing.) We went inside and ordered; because he has celiac disease, he can't eat wheat, so he ordered a baked potato and a hamburger with no bun. We sat down to eat and he looked down at his burger patty and said, "Mmmmm...steak."

SHHH!

We decided to meet up at the pizza place for lunch, which was good because I was starving. When we met there, he informed me that he had already eaten, and insisted we head to a local bookstore, over a mile walk. There, we spent the next two hours reading books. In absolute silence. Every time I tried to ask him a question or start a conversation, he'd give a one-word reply and go back to reading. Not that I could hear him, anyway, because my stomach was growling so loudly.

FINE DINING

I asked where he wanted to go to lunch, and he said he had just the place in mind. We were in Manhattan, where there are thousands of cute, inexpensive places to eat, but he was set on walking us to his pick. It was a grocery store, where he enthusiastically recommended the chicken soup from the salad bar.

INDIAN BUMMER

I met him at a friend's party, and he asked me out, saying he wanted to surprise me for dinner. On the way there, he told me we were going for Indian food (I have an irritable stomach, so it's not my favorite, but I planned to just eat some plain naan bread). When we walked in, everyone greeted him ecstatically…because his family owns the restaurant. So on our first date, I had to meet his mom, dad, aunts, cousins, and grandfather. I told them I couldn't eat spicy food, but they kept bringing me dishes and begging me to try them, so I kept nibbling to be polite. Of course, before we could leave, I got terrible stomach cramps and rushed to the bathroom. If that wasn't embarrassing enough, when I came out, his mother handed me a Pepto-Bismol.

DENNY'S DREAMBOAT

He picked me up and took me to dinner…at Denny's. I remained calm. We sat down and looked at our menus, and I told him I felt like having a hamburger. When the waitress came by, he ordered the same thing for both of us: the cheapest breakfast meal. He then proceeded to argue with her about how the same meal was twenty cents more at dinnertime than in the morning, and demanded the morning price. After she walked away, I sat there, stunned. My date yelled, "Awkward silence!"

HE'S HOT DOGGIN'

For our first date, we went to an outdoor bar along the boardwalk for a late afternoon drink. After two margaritas, the date was going fine and I started getting hungry—I was hoping it would lead into dinner together. The bar owner picked up the microphone and announced they were starting a hot-dog-eating contest, and my date looked at me, raised his eyebrows, and ran up to the stage. Uhh, what? He then started hooting and pounding on his chest like a gorilla. I sat there speechless while I watched him shove hot dog after hot dog in his mouth—his face was all red and he had pieces of wet bun (he dunked the dogs in soda first, I guess to get them down more easily) stuck to his face. He actually came in second place, which he thought was pretty impressive when he came back to the table. I'd lost my appetite for dinner—and a second date.

THE IRON CHEF

A very cute and buff guy invited me over to his place, saying he wanted to cook me dinner. When I got there, he pulled out some frozen tamales and popped them in the microwave. He served them on paper plates along with tap water in giant plastic cups. He ate his in under thirty seconds and then began to go on and on about how slowly I ate and how he couldn't believe I wasn't finished yet. He was getting more and more irritated and stood behind me waiting for me to finish so he could clean up.

Awful First Dates: Hollywood Dispatch

"I went on one blind date, and after that I never, ever did again. The guy repeated everything he said twice. He'd say, 'So, how are you? How are you?' and I'd say I was fine, and he'd say, 'Good, good.' Or 'I'll have the mac n' cheese, please. Yeah, the mac n' cheese.' I don't know if there was something actually wrong with him or if it was just a bad habit, but no more blind dates after that."

—singer Eliza Doolittle

Chapter 11

MISS "IT'S NOT YOU, IT'S ME. NO, REALLY."

n every dating disaster you've read up until this point, it was always the other person's fault. It would be so much easier to end the book here and pretend that men are the problem, and that our personality flaws, freak-outs, and screw-ups never jeopardized anything with the guy who could've been the one. Well, we're only human. Just like the guys you've read about, women occasionally do something weird, say something stupid, read too much into who pays, or get way too drunk—or sometimes pull all of these in one night. Sorry, boys.

For example, one guy wrote in about this psycho hose-beast:

"I met a girl at a birthday party and sparks flew, so I asked her out for a drink afterward. Halfway through the night, she asked me about 'the status of our relationship.' I stammered that we were just having our first drink and that we should perhaps not call it a relationship yet. When she heard that, she started shaking, crying, and screaming. She yelled that I'd wasted her time and stormed out. I asked for the check and was paying when she stormed back in, swearing at me. I ignored her and walked out to my car—she followed me, and when I unlocked the doors, she jumped in and refused to get out, demanding to know why I wouldn't date her. When I eventually got her out of the car, she called me repeatedly until 2 a.m., begging me to sleep with her and asking why I didn't love her when it was so obviously right. My favorite part was when, in the bar, she stopped midscream, adopted an air of exaggerated patience, and started miming taking something out of a bag and placing it on her head. I was completely flummoxed until she explained that she was 'putting on her psychologist's hat' and suggested that I was being held back by fear. She was right…the fear that she'd break into my house and decapitate my pets!"

Yes, that chick should probably seek out the nearest psych ward. The other ladies in this chapter's offenses don't require electro-shock therapy—but they are enough for the offenders to just hang their pretty heads and say "my bad" (on second thought, no one except for characters on *The Real World* circa 2002 should ever say "my bad").

THE CHARDONNAY CHUGGER

I was really nervous for my superhot online date and over-compensated by downing a bottle of wine before I went to meet him. By the time I got to the classy wine bar he'd picked, I was completely drunk and ended up puking for over an hour and then passing out on the bathroom floor. My date carried me to a cab, but I was too incoherent to even tell him where I lived, so he took my cell phone and called the only number he knew would give him my address—my mom.

STRESSED—AND UNDERDRESSED

We were supposed to meet at a cute restaurant in my neighborhood at 7:30 that night. I went out to walk my dog, leaving just enough time to shower, do my hair and makeup, and change into a dress and heels when I got back. But when I got home, I realized I'd left my keys inside and locked myself out. I called a friend with the spare, but she couldn't be there for an hour. Rather than stand him up, I texted him with the situation and—to my total embarrassment—he wanted to come meet me. He showed up at my front steps all ready for our date, and I was in a ratty T-shirt and jean shorts. He handled it well, but it wasn't exactly the first impression I wanted to make.

INTERNATIONAL EXPERIENCE

I was taking a trip to Dublin and met a really great guy next to me on the plane. When our flight got in, we had an incredible first date—so incredible that it ended the next morning. As I was walking home—totally disheveled and wearing four-inch heels—along a historic, cobblestoned street, I heard a bunch of people laughing. I looked up and saw a bus full of tourists wearing Viking hats. Their guide, who was pointing out the sites on a microphone, had spotted me and was telling them: "And on your left is a local girl doing the 'Walk of Shame' after a long night out…"

CLEANUP, AISLE THREE!

We went to a hockey game, where I had quite a few drinks, and then out to dinner. When we got back to his house, I threw up all over his floor, and then I peed myself. I have never been more mortified, especially because I drink often and I've never lost bladder control. So while he kindly cleaned everything up, I swore at him and accused him of drugging me, since that was *obviously* the only reason I could come up with for embarrassing myself so much.

NOT SANTA'S LITTLE HELPER

Last December, I saw a guy dressed as Santa at the bar—we spent a few hours talking and making out, so I invited him over. We started to make out at my house but were both really drunk, and he passed out. I tried to put his cell phone on the nightstand but dropped it, smashing the screen and making the back piece shoot off, lost somewhere under the bed. In the morning, when he was walking out the door, I handed him his phone, and he started cussing. Luckily, I closed the door and never saw him again, but I did find a stray Santa boot under my bed with some cell phone pieces.

HOT FOR HIM

I was on one of those awkward, what-do-we-have-in-common first dates where both of us were grasping at conversational straws. Trying to be a little flirtatious, I took my long hair down from a ponytail and flipped it. The folks at the table behind ours then tapped me on the shoulder and said, "Um, miss? Your hair is on fire." Which it was; the end had singed on their candle. After I put it out, the entire cafe smelled like burned hair, but I tried to laugh it off with the guy. But we still didn't have anything to talk about—even setting myself on fire hadn't broken the ice with this guy.

DR. STRANGESMELL

He was intelligent, sweet, and lovely. We were having such a great time at dinner that we decided to continue on to a bar. We were getting cozy in a little booth, tucked away from everyone else, and got into an extremely intense conversation. Right in the middle of me saying something "important," despite my best efforts to control it, I let out a silent but absolutely stinking fart. It lingered, and there was no one else around to possibly blame it on. I was so embarrassed that I just wanted to get away, so I hailed the first cab I could find, hastily cheek-kissed, hopped in, and left. The next day I realized I should get over myself, so I wrote him about going out again, but I never heard back.

THE GOOGLE STALKER

I met a friend of a friend at a bar, went home, and Googled the crap out of him. His name plus every damn thing I knew about him as a second search term: his name AND ice hockey; his name AND his alma mater; etc. We go on our date and have a wonderful time, during which we flirtatiously quibble over something trivial that we decide must be Googled immediately. We return to my apartment, he types in the trivial quibble…and in the Google dropdown list of the recently searched terms is his name fifteen times. He never called me again.

SHE'S GOTTA GO

I could tell it was a wonderful date because I didn't want to go home—every time we said we should get the check, we ended up talking for another few minutes, then saying we should go, then talking again. We'd been so deep in conversation that I suddenly realized I had to pee…bad. He offered to walk me home, and since I lived close by, I decided not to break the momentum by excusing myself to the ladies' room and would just go in ten minutes when I got home. Of course, the walk was just as conversation-packed and meandering. Once we got to my front door, I was in so much pain that I was actually hurrying him and giving one-word answers so I could get inside. He finally realized I was trying to wrap it up, and when he leaned in to kiss me good night, I finally couldn't take it anymore and I just started peeing.

ACCIDENTS HAPPEN

On my way to the date, someone hit my car and fled the scene. Though my car was totaled, I managed to get my roommate to come get me after the police left and drop me off at the restaurant. Because I didn't want to be a drama queen or worry him, since I felt okay, I didn't mention any of this to my date. However, my nerves were shaken, so I drank more than I usually would to calm down. At one point he went to touch my knee, and to my horror I realized I must have injured it in the wreck, as apparently while we were sitting there, the wound started to bleed through my jeans. With the heavy drinking, the bloody knee I hadn't noticed, and the fact that my roommate dropped me off, my date decided I had a drinking problem and even after I explained what happened, he didn't return my call.

ROMANCE AND RACCOONS

The building I lived in had a severe raccoon problem. (This was especially irritating since my landlord did nothing about it, yet owned a pest control company.) After drinks with a super cute guy, we ended up sitting outside on the porch swing together, looking up at the stars. It was really romantic, and of course I hadn't warned my date about the raccoon infestation, because what girl in her right mind would? We heard a rustling sound, and my date jumped off the seat and yelled, "What *is* that?!" Knowing exactly what it was, I grabbed a big stick to try to scare the raccoon off. The thing hissed at me as I jabbed at it to make it run away. But since its mouth was open wide and I couldn't exactly see, I accidentally speared the thing right through the mouth. I started screaming and my roommates ran outside as the raccoon ran off. That's when I looked around for my date—and he was running to his car and driving away. I never heard from him again, but the various raccoons hung around all year.

THE HALLOWEEN WEENIE

We'd been chatting on email and he suggested we meet up for the first time at his friend's Halloween party. I told him I'd be easy to recognize: I can't stand when girls dress up as sexy nurses or sexy cats, so I'd be the one wearing a giant hot dog costume. I guess he thought I was joking, because he didn't bother to tell me that no one at the party was dressing up…which I realized immediately when I arrived in costume, barely fitting my bun through the door, and saw the horrified look on his (and everyone else's) face.

THE LUKE AND LEIA EFFECT

He took me to a huge, elaborate dance party for the company he worked for, and he even sprung for a limo for our double date. He was cute and smart and sweet and hilarious, and we absolutely shredded that dance floor. Still, all night I had a creepy feeling that something was off. I didn't figure it out until he took me home. As he leaned in to kiss me, I realized that he was a dead ringer for my brother, so I pushed him back and ran out of there.

THAR SHE BLOWS!

We'd been friends for a while and I'd had a crush on him, so when he asked me out, I was so happy. We went out for beer and pizza, and then went back to his apartment. He started kissing me, and the combination of booze, greasy food, and excitement over this finally actually happening did me in, I guess, because I started throwing up—into his mouth. I reeled back and covered my mouth with my hands, but it was still coming up. I ran to his bathroom, finished throwing up, and then cleaned myself up at the sink. I went back to his room and found him stripping the sheets and wiping his face with his shirt; I'd covered him and half his room in our dinner.

Awful First Dates: Hollywood Dispatch

"My first date with my husband started badly. I didn't know it was a date. I thought I was going to an event, and then there was just one person at it. I was set up by friends to think I was going to an event, because they knew I wouldn't go on a date. I was angry. And he didn't know, because he thought I knew I was coming just to meet him. It started out really badly. But as you can see, it ended happy."

—Salma Hayek

CONCLUSION

After hearing hundreds of bad date stories, one of the things that most surprised me was that, once in a long while, a bad date can turn into a good relationship. Take Salma Hayek's story—she met her date because her friends duped her, so she spent the beginning of the date steaming mad. Eventually, the man became her husband and father of her child. My own parents, who have been happily married for forty years, actually met on what my mother would consider to be a bad first date. My mom says her date was dull and that they didn't have any chemistry. So how did she end up married, based on that night? She was on a double date—and fell for her friend's date instead (my dad).

But let's face it: most bad first dates don't lead to

happily-ever-afters. They're usually awkward, embarrass-ing, painful, or feel like a total waste of time. (I've left many a first date mumbling, "I put on makeup for this?") But I do see a few upsides of bad dates. They make you apprecia-tive of regular old uneventful-but-meh dates, since at least nothing horrible happened. Going out to dinner or a drink with a sociopath makes me more appreciative of times I'm actually having fun, like doing those same activities with dear friends. Hell, I've had dinner at posh restaurants with guys who turned out to be such weirdos that the next night I was thanking the lord to be sitting alone on my couch eating Cinnamon Toast Crunch for dinner.

More than anything, bad dates bond us together. Because they're so awful, they give you a greater apprecia-tion for the good first dates. They bond women and men, because when you have fun and you're out with a normal, nice guy, the flashbacks of weirdos past might make you want to hang onto him by the lapels and shout, "Thank goodness you're here!" (Don't actually try this—then *you'll* be the awful first date.) Awful first dates also bond us with other women; they give us something to laugh about and inspire a fun one-upping of "No, I have a *worse* date" com-petitions. Awful first-date stories are a common ground we can use to bridge divides, since whether you're single or married, no matter your age or where you're from—unless you're Cindy Crawford—you've probably had one. And even if it wasn't fun at the time, I bet it's a funny story now.

"I went on a nice first date where this guy took me to a park and he brought a picnic, a backgammon board, and a blanket—it was a really great way to get to know someone in a relaxed atmosphere rather than stuffy dinner to kind of loosen things up. I've been on bad dates, but I don't want to think about those!"

—Padma Lakshmi

ACKNOWLEDGMENTS

ore than anyone else, I need to thank my parents: I am convinced that observing your forty-year marriage, in which you still hold hands when no one's looking, is the reason that anything else seems like settling. My Grandma Wex, who told everyone from her hairdresser to her waitress the title of this book, and who's only asked me if I'm dating someone yet roughly every week for the past ten years. Becca Shapiro, my awful first dates conspirator—I wish we could write off all those Cherry Coke Zeros we drank while talking about men as a business expense; I know that your very own Cal Ripken-Woody Allen hybrid is on his way. Kate McKean of Howard Morhaim Literary Agency, who's supertough but also so warm and reassuring that she makes me want to coin a term for a friend-agent (fragent?). Shana Drehs, my wonderful editor at Sourcebooks, for her talent, flexibility, and encouragement. Linda Wells at *Allure*, Joanna Coles at *Marie Claire*, and Lucy Kaylin at *O, The Oprah Magazine*, for encouraging my writing along the way and making me infinitely better at it.

I couldn't have laughed about these stories without my cabal of sympathetic (and often empathetic) smartass girlfriends, including but not limited to Amber Herczeg, Rachel Sturtz, Jess Dove, Sue Carris, Wendi Hausfeld-Carragher—and Peter Martin, who I talk to like he's a girlfriend, much to his chagrin. I promise never to tell which stories belong to whom. Lena Green, for her great illustrations, and for agreeing to help with this book when it seemed like the only payment would be in unlimited bottles of nail polish. Julia Scirrotto and Juno DeMelo, for inspiring me with their willingness to go on international first dates. Sergio Kletnoy, the Power Serge, for helping wrangle celebrities. Jeanne Marie Laskas, who somehow always makes writing look easy. Thanks to awesome copy editor Lani Meyer, who is responsible for all errors in my last book but none of these ones. Ginsberg, the dog who is always waiting up when I get home from a date and is always trying to remind me not to analyze things so much.

Thanks to all of the brave daters who shared stories, or at least weighed in on other people's stories, on www.awfulfirstdates.com.

To all of the guys who took me on dates, some even while knowing I was writing a book about bad ones: thanks for being good sports. To the ones who weren't good sports: thanks for being good material. To the guys who took me on good first dates and then disappeared: eat it. And to the next guy out there who's going to take me on an *awesome* first date: call me.

ABOUT THE AUTHOR

Sarah Z. Wexler is the author of *Living Large: From SUVs to Double Ds: Why Going Bigger Isn't Going Better*. Her writing has been published in *Esquire*, *Wired*, *Martha Stewart Living*, *SELF*, *The Washington Post Magazine*, *The New York Post*, *Marie Claire*, *Food Network Magazine*, *Popular Science*, *Allure*, *Redbook*, and *Ladies' Home Journal*. She holds an MFA in creative nonfiction writing from the University of Pittsburgh. She lives, and goes on first dates, in New York City.